Planning for Learning through
The Seasons

by Rachel Sparks Linfield and Penny Coltman
Illustrated by Cathy Hughes

Contents

About the book

This bumper collection offers a term's worth of planning on each of the four seasons: Spring, Summer, Autumn and Winter. Each season is divided into themed weeks, in which every activity links to one of the Early Learning Goals, a guide to which you will find at the beginning of this book. In each topic you'll also find a skills overview, photocopiable pages to give to parents, a list of all the resources you'll need and ideas for bringing the topic together. So, whatever the time of year, you'll always have planned activities ready!

Published by Practical Pre-School Books

A Division of MA Education, St Jude's Church, Dulwich Road, Herne Hill, London, SE24 0PB Tel. 020 7738 5454

© Practical Pre-School Books 2009

Planning for Learning Through the Seasons ISBN: 978-1-90457-597-9

www.practicalpreschoolbooks.com

Making plans

Why plan?

The purpose of planning is to make sure that all children enjoy a broad and balanced curriculum. All planning should be useful. Plans are working documents which you spend time preparing, but which should later repay your efforts. Try to be concise. This will help you in finding information quickly when you need it.

Long term plans

Preparing a long-term plan, which maps out the curriculum during a year or even two, will help you to ensure that you are providing a variety of activities and are meeting the statutory requirements of the *Statutory Framework for the Early Years Foundation Stage* (2007).

Your long-term plan need not be detailed. Divide the time period over which you are planning into fairly equal sections, such as half terms. Choose a topic for each section. Young children benefit from making links between the new ideas they encounter so as you select each topic, think about the time of year in which you plan to do it.

Although each topic will address all the learning areas, some could focus on a specific area. For example, a topic on Spring lends itself well to activities relating to knowledge and understanding of the living world. Another topic might particularly encourage the appreciation of stories. Try to make sure that you provide a variety of topics in your long-term plans.

Autumn 1	Me and my family
Autumn 2	Winter
Spring 1	Fairy Tales
Spring 2	Spring
Summer 1	Opposites
Summer 2	Summer

Medium term plans

Medium term plans will outline the contents of a topic in a little more detail. One way to start this process is by brainstorming on a large piece of paper. Work with your team writing down all the activities you can think of which are relevant to the topic. As you do this it may become clear that some activities go well together. Think about dividing them into themes, the topic of Spring for example has themes such as detecting Spring, frogs and Spring rain.

At this stage it is helpful to make a chart. Write the theme ideas down the side of the chart and put a different area of learning at the top of each column. Now you can insert your brainstormed ideas and will quickly see where there are gaps. As you complete the chart take account of children's earlier experiences and provide opportunities for them to progress.

Refer back to the Statutory Framework document and check that you have addressed as many different aspects of it as you can. Once all your medium-term plans are complete make sure that there are no neglected areas.

Day to day plans

The plans you make for each day will outline aspects such as:

- resources needed;
- the way in which you might introduce activities;
- the organisation of adult help;

Making plans

- safety;
- size of the group;
- individual needs;
- timing.

Identify the learning and ELGs which each activity is intended to promote. Make a note of any assessments or observations which you are likely to carry out. After using the plans make notes of which activities were particularly successful, or any changes you would make another time.

A final note

Planning should be seen as flexible. Not all groups meet every day, and not all children attend every day. Any part of the plans in this book can be used independently, stretched over a longer period or condensed to meet the needs of any group. You will almost certainly adapt the activities as children respond to them in different ways and bring their own ideas, interests and enthusiasms. Be prepared to be flexible over timing as some ideas prove more popular than others. The important thing is to ensure that the children are provided with a varied and enjoyable curriculum which meets their individual developing needs.

Using the book

- Collect or prepare suggested resources for each topic. These are listed on the following pages: Spring page 21, Summer page , Autumn page and Winter page
- Read the section which outlines links to the Early Learning Goals (pages 5-8) and explains the rationale for the topics of Spring, Summer, Autumn and Winter.
- For each weekly theme two activities are described in detail as examples to help you in your planning and preparation. Key vocabulary, questions and learning opportunities are identified.
- The skills chart at the end of each topic will help you to see at a glance which aspects of children's development are being addressed as a focus each week.
- As children take part in the topic activities, their learning will progress. Collecting evidence at the

end of the book explains how you might monitor children's achievements.
- Find out on in the 'Bringing It All Together' pages how each topic can be brought together in a grand finale involving parents, children and friends.
- There is additional material to support the working partnership of families and children in the form of a home links page, and a photocopiable parent's page found at the end of each topic.

It is important to appreciate that the ideas presented in this book will only be a part of your planning. Many activities which will be taking place as routine in your group may not be mentioned. For example, it is assumed that sand, dough, water, puzzles, floor toys and large scale apparatus are part of the Early Years Foundation Stage. Role play areas, stories, rhymes and singing, and group discussion times are similarly assumed to behappening in each week although they may not be a focus for described activities. Groups should also ensure that there is a balance of adult-led and child-initiated actiities.

Using this book in Northern Ireland, Scotland and Wales

The activites in this book are appropriate for use throughout the United Kingdom. They are designed to promote the development of early skills and to represent good practice in the early years.

Although the curriculum guidelines in Northern Ireland, Scotland and Wales differ, they all adress similar areas of learning, and comparable references to the Early Years Foundation Stage Early Learning Goals can be found.

Glossary

EYFS: Early Years Foundation Stage
ELG: Early Learning Goal

Using the 'Early Learning Goals'

Having decided on your topic and made your medium term plans you can use the Early Learning Goals to highlight the key learning opportunities your activities will address. The desirable outcomes are split into six areas: Personal and Social Development, Communication, Language and Literacy, Problem Solving, Reasoning and Numeracy, Knowledge and Understanding of the World, Physical Development and Creative Development. Do not expect each of your topics to cover every outcome but your long-term plans should allow for all the outcomes to be addressed.

The following section lists the Early Learning Goals to show what children are expected to be able to do by the time they enter compulsory education in each area of learning. These points will be used throughout this book to show how activities for a topic on each of the seasons links to these expectations. For example, Personal and Social Development point 8 includes 'work as part of a group and independently'. Activities suggested which provide the opportunity for children to do this will have the reference PS2. This will enable you to see which parts of the desirable outcomes are covered in a given week and plan for areas to be revisited and developed.

In addition you can ensure that activities offer variety in the outcomes to be encountered. Often a similar activity may be carried out to achieve different learning outcomes. For example, when going on a walk to detect signs of Winter children will be able to develop aspects of Knowledge and Understanding of the World. They can also be encouraged to work as a group, to explore new learning and to treat living things and the environment with care. In this way children will at the same time be furthering their Personal and Social Development. It is important therefore that activities have clearly defined learning outcomes so that these may be emphasised during the activity and for recording purposes.

Personal, Social and Emotional Development (PS)

These outcomes consider important aspects of development which affect the ways children learn, behave and relate to others.

By the end of the EYFS children should:

PS1 Continue to be interested, excited and motivated to learn.

PS2 Be confident to try new activities, initiate ideas and speak in a familiar group.

PS3 Maintain attention, concentrate, and sit quietly when appropriate.

PS4 Respond to significant experiences, showing a range of feelings when appropriate.

PS5 Have a developing awareness of their own needs, views and feelings, and be sensitive to the needs, views and feelings of others.

PS6 Have a developing respect for their own cultures and beliefs and those of other people.

PS7 Form good relationships with peers and adults.

PS8 Work as part of a group or class taking turns and sharing fairly; understanding that there need to be agreed values and codes of behaviour for groups of people, including adults and children, to work harmoniously.

PS9 Understand what is right, what is wrong and why.

PS10 Consider the consequences of their words and actions for themselves and others.

PS11 Dress and undress independently and manage their own personal hygiene.

PS12 Select and use activities and resources independently.

PS13 Understand that people have different needs, views, cultures and beliefs that need to be treated with respect.

PS14 Understand that they can expect others to treat their needs, views, cultures and beliefs with respect.

Spring
The topic of Spring provides valuable opportunities for children to treat living things properly and to show concern for their local environment. Children will be encouraged to be sensitive to the needs and feelings of others by activities which involve thinking of carers around the time of Mothers' Day. Inevitably many outcomes will also develop as a natural result of activities in other key areas. For example, when children collaborate to play games within Problem 0Solving, Reasoning and Numeracy and Physical Development they will also have the opportunity to further PS8.

Summer

The topic of Summer provides valuable opportunities for children to show sensitivity to their surroundings, to work collaboratively and to express feelings in response to natural objects. As children become more aware of the changes which take place in summer they have the chance to explore new learning and develop ideas. In addition, many of the outcomes for Personal, Social and Emotional Development will develop as a natural result of activities in other key areas. For example, when children play games within Physical Development they will also have the opportunity to further PS8.

Autumn

The topic of Autumn provides valuable opportunities for children to show sensitivity to their surroundings, to work collaboratively and to express feelings in response to natural objects. As children become more aware of the changes which take place in Autumn they have the chance to explore new learning such as caring for their environment when out on an 'Autumn walk' and to develop ideas such as talking about favourite Autumn fruits and recognising that others have different favourites. Also, many of the outcomes for Personal, Social and Emotional Development will develop as a natural result of activities in other key areas, for example when children play some of the suggested Autumn games within Physical Development they will also have the opportunity to work as part of a group and to take turns and share fairly (PS8).

Winter

The topic of Winter provides valuable opportunities for children to treat living things properly and to show concern for their local environment. Through thinking of birds and feeding them during the Winter months children will be sensitive to the needs of others. Many of the areas outlined above will be covered on an almost incidental basis as children carry out the activities described for the other areas of learning. For example, when children play games and join in with number rhymes they will also be learning to play collaboratively.

Communication Language and Literacy (L)

By the end of the EYFS children should:

L1   Interact with others, negotiating plans and activities and taking turns in conversation.

L2   Enjoy listening to and using spoken and written language, and readily turn to it in their play and learning.

L3   Sustain attentive listening, responding to what they have heard with relevant comments, questions or actions.

L4   Listen with enjoyment and respond to stories, songs and other music, rhymes and poems and make up their own stories, songs, rhymes and poems.

L5   Extend their vocabulary, exploring the meanings and sounds of new words.

L6   Speak clearly and audibly with confidence and control and show awareness of the listener.

L7   Use language to imagine and recreate roles and experiences .

L8   Use talk to organise, sequence and clarify thinking, ideas, feelings and events.

L9   Hear and say sounds in words in the order in which they occur.

L10   Link sounds to letters, naming and sounding the letters of the alphabet.

L11   Use their phonic knowledge to write simple regular words and make phonetically plausible attempts at more complex words.

L12   Explore and experiment with sounds, words and texts.

L13   Retell narratives in the correct sequence, drawing on language patterns of stories.

L14   Read a range of familiar and common words and simple sentences independently.

L15   Know that print carries meaning and, in English, is read from left to right and top to bottom.

L16   Show an understanding of the elements of stories, such as main character, sequence of events and openings and how information can be found in non-fiction texts to answer questions about where, who, why and how.

L17   Attempt writing for various purposes, using features of different forms such as lists, stories and instructions.

L18   Write their own names and other things such as labels and captions, and begin to form simple sentences, sometimes using punctuation.

L19   Use a pencil and hold it effectively to form recognisable letters, most of which are correctly formed.

Spring

The activities suggested for the topic of Spring provide the opportunity for children to respond to a variety of imaginative situations including stories and role play. Through looking at books and listening to stories such as *The Very Hungry Caterpillar* and *Five Minutes' Peace* children will be able to respond to and enjoy books. The making of group big books will enable them to know how books are organised. The writing of greetings for cards and name labels for pictures will help children to develop their early writing skills. Throughout all the activities children will be encouraged to communicate fluently and with meaning.

Summer

The activities suggested for the theme of Summer include several in which children describe observations and events, reinforcing and extending their vocabulary. There are opportunities for role play as children respond to sounds, stories, poems and ideas. Creating a travel agent's role-play area will allow children to use their imagination. Throughout the topic opportunities are described in which children explore the sounds of words and see some of their ideas recorded in both pictures and print.

Autumn

Many of the Autumn activities suggested encourage children to describe observations and events, reinforcing and extending their vocabulary. There are opportunities for role play as children respond to Autumn sounds, stories, poems and ideas. Making and enjoying a tree-house role-play area will allow children to use their imagination. Throughout the topic there are opportunities for children to explore the sounds of words and to see some of their ideas recorded in both pictures and print.

Winter

The activities suggested for the topic of Winter provide the opportunity for children to respond to a variety of imaginative situations including stories and role play. The writing of labels for displays and the Winter menus will help children to develop their early writing skills which may start with pictures and progress to beginning to form letters. Throughout all the activities children will be encouraged to communicate fluently and with meaning.

Problem Solving, Reasoning and Numeracy (N)

By then end of the EYFS children should:

N1   Say and use number names in order in familiar contexts.

N2   Count reliably up to ten everyday objects.

N3   Recognise numerals 1 to 9.

N4   use developing mathematical ideas and methods to solve practical problems.

N5   In practical activities and discussion, begin to use the vocabulary involved in adding and subtracting.

N6   Use language such as 'more' or 'less' to compare two numbers.

N7   Find one more or one less than a number from one to ten.

N8   Begin to relate addition to combining two groups of objects and subtraction to 'taking away'.

N9   Use language such as 'greater', 'smaller', heavier' or 'lighter' to compare quantities.

N10   Talk about, recognise and recreate simple patterns.

N11   Use language such as 'circle' or 'bigger' to describe the shape and size of solids and flat shapes.

N12   Use everyday words to describe position

Spring

As children carry out the activities on the topic of Spring, seasonal artefacts, songs and images are used to introduce and reinforce the fundamental counting skills of number awareness and one-to-one matching. The development of mathematical vocabulary is a priority and the importance of encouraging children to talk about their first-hand experiences is emphasised throughout the topic. Through water play children explore aspects of capacity. Measurement and pattern are similarly encountered in relevant contexts.

Summer

The theme of Summer provides a meaningful context for mathematical activities which are closely linked to everyday experiences. Natural materials such

as flowers and fruits provide opportunities for children to sort by size, colour and shape. Using these materials in slightly different ways encourages children to develop comparative and positional language. Simple activities, such as ordering a row of flowers by size, provide a wealth of language opportunities as well as a context for counting. Daisies can also be used as a non-standard unit for measuring length.

Autumn

Use the theme of Autumn to try activities that have a meaningful context and link to the children's everyday experiences. For example, use natural materials such as leaves and autumn fruits for sorting activities - by size, colour and shape. Using these materials in slightly different ways encourages children to develop comparative and positional language. Simple activities such as ordering a row of conkers by size provide a wealth of language opportunities as well as a context for counting. Conkers can also be used as a non standard unit for measuring weight and length.

Winter

In this topic there are several cooking activities that provide wonderful opportunities to talk about amounts and numbers, and to solve simple problems in a real context. As you make bread, for example, encourage children to count ingredients by the spoonful as you add them, to describe the shape of the dough ball and to talk about how it can be made to change shape. Count the balls of dough. Decide whether or not there will be enough for one or two rolls each.

Knowledge and Understanding of the World (K)

By the end of the EYFS children should:

K1   Investigate objects and materials by using all of their senses as appropriate.

K2   Find out about, and identify, some features of living things, objects and events they observe.

K3   Look closely at similarities, differences, patterns and change.

K4   Ask questions about why things happen and how things work.

K5   Build and construct with a wide range of objects, selecting appropriate resources and adapting their work where necessary.

K6   Select the tools and techniques they need to shape, assemble and join materials they are using.

K7   Find out about and identify the uses of everyday technology and use information and communication technology and programmable toys to support their learning.

K8   Find out about past and present events in their own lives, and in those of their families and other people they know observe.

K9   Find out about and identify features in the place they live and the natural world.

K10   Find out about their environment, and talk about those features they like and dislike.

K11   Begin to know about their own cultures and beliefs and those of other people.

Spring

The topic of Spring provides ample opportunity for children to explore and recognise features of living things. Activities which relate to both the natural and the made world will encourage children to look at similarities and differences. Children will further their ability to use skills such as cutting, joining and building through making nests and cress bonnets. Throughout all the activities children should be given the chance to talk about their observations and to ask questions.

Summer

The topic of Summer provides opportunities to help children experience K2, 3, 4 and 9. In addition they will touch on K5, 6 and 10. For example, as children go on a walk to detect signs of summer they will also talk about where they live and the local environment. When making marble minibeasts they will select resources.

Autumn

The topic of Autumn provides opportunities to help children experience K2, 3, 5 and 6. In addition they will touch on K1 and 8. For example, as childrengo on an Autumn walk to detect signs of Autumn they will also talk about where they live and the local environment.

Winter

The topic of Winter provides ample opportunity for children to explore and recognise features of living things. Activities which relate to both the natural and the made world will encourage children to look at similarities and differences. Observation is a strong element of the topic with children watching birds feeding, changes occurring through cooking and ice melting. Throughout all the activities children should be given the chance to talk about their experiences and to ask questions.

Physical Development (PD)

By the end of the EYFS children should:

PD1   Move with confidence, imagination and in safety.

PD2   Move with control and coordination.

PD3   Travel around, under, over and through balancing and climbing equipment.

PD4   Show awareness of space, of themselves and of others.

PD5   Recognise the importance of keeping healthy and those things which contribute to this.

PD6   Recognise the changes that happen to their bodies when they are active.

PD7   Use a range of small and large equipment

PD8   Handle tools, objects, construction and malleable materials safely and with increasing control.

Spring

Activities involving mime and dance are used thematically to support children's developing abilities to express their ideas and feelings through movement in the topic of Spring. Gross motor skills are also encouraged through games and the use of large apparatus. As children manipulate materials in a variety of 'making' activities they will develop fine muscle control and co-ordination.

Summer

Activities such as moving marble minibeasts or playing with bats and balls will offer experience of PD5. Through the activities associated with the sports day children can develop control and coordination while also having the opportunity to work both collaboratively and independently. Children will become aware of the restriction of space and the needs of others by playing whole group games.

Autumn

Activities such as printing with leaves or blow painting during the Windy Week will offer experience of P2. Through being imaginary kites, seeds, harvesting machines and squirrels children can develop control and co-ordination while also having the opportunity to work in an imaginative way. By playing whole group games children will become aware of the restriction of space and the needs of others.

Winter

Activities involving mime and dance are used thematically to support children's developing abilities to express their ideas and feelings through movement in the topic of Spring. Gross motor skills are also encouraged through games and the use of large apparatus. As children manipulate materials in a variety of 'making' activities they will develop fine muscle control and co-ordination.

Creative Development (C)

By the end of the EYFS children should:

C1   Respond in a variety of ways to what they see, hear, smell, touch and feel.

C2   Express and communicate their ideas, thoughts and feelings by using a widening range of materials, suitable tools, imaginative and role-play, movement, designing and making, and a variety of songs and musical instruments.

C3   Explore colour, texture, shape, form and space in two or three dimensions.

C4   Recognise and explore how sounds can be changed, sing simple songs from memory, recognise repeated sounds and sound patterns and match movements to music.

C5   Use their imagination in art and design, music, dance, imaginative and role play and stories.

Spring

During this topic children will experience working with a variety of materials as they make models, prepare some seasonal edible treats and explore a range of art and craft activities. Close observation is encouraged with children recording their ideas using a variety of media. Model ponds, for example, are constructed collaboratively using everyday recycled materials. Weather conditions are used to stimulate imaginative responses with children making their own sounds to imitate spring showers.

Summer

During this topic children will experience working with a variety of materials as they make models, such as making a model caravan in the summer holiday week, and explore a range of art and craft activities. Poetry and stories are used to inspire imaginative responses, for example travelling on a 'magic carpet' to imaginary or real holiday destinations.

Autumn

During this topic children will experience working with a variety of materials as they bake Autumn recipes, make models and explore a range of art and craft activities. Cooking is particularly effective in stimulating sensory observations as children feel the sticky dough, smell the baking bread or taste the still warm gingerbread biscuits. Poetry, stories and weather conditions are used as the basis of imaginative responses, for example children listen to a poem about the wind, watch streamers blowing outside and then move and dance like kites.

Winter

During this topic children will experience working with a variety of materials as they make models, prepare seasonal edible treats and explore a range of art and craft activities. Close observation is encouraged with children recording their ideas using a variety of media. Children will develop awareness of shape, form and space as they handle equipment, cut, join and explore materials. Ideas are expressed through a variety of media including paint, chalks and collage.

SPRING

Topic Contents

Week 1
Detecting spring

Personal, Social and Emotional Development

● Look at a large picture of a Spring-time scene (trees in blossom, Spring flowers, children playing outside). Discuss what children can do in Spring that they cannot do in Winter. Talk about how children feel in the Spring. What are their favourite activities? (PS4)

● Discuss festivals which children in the group celebrate during Spring. These might include Easter (Christian), Baisakhi (Sikh), Holi (Hindu), Passover (Jewish). Invite parents to come and talk to children about the celebrations. (PS13, 14)

Communication, Language and Literacy

● Read *The Very Hungry Caterpillar* by Eric Carle. Make a group version based on children's favourite foods. (L1, 8, 13)

● In preparation for the Physical Development activity based on bulbs read *The Tiny Seed* by Eric Carle. Talk about the changes that took place. Discuss the differences between Spring and Winter and Spring and Summer. (L7, 8)

● Make a spring picnic role play area. Securely fix a tight string at ceiling height across a corner of the room. Cut across an unopened roll of green crepe paper every 1-2 cm. Without unrolling these sections encourage the children to help you to twist them. Then shake them open to make long twisty fronds. Dangle these from the string, packing them fairly closely, and introducing paler greens, pinks and whites. The end result is a weeping blossom tree which encloses an area. Place a picnic rug and tea set on the floor. Children love the feel of moving through the tree curtain to reach this special place. (L1)

Problem Solving, Reasoning and Numeracy

● Use the group's version of The Very Hungry Caterpillar to practise counting. Ask questions such as 'How many apples did the caterpillar eat?' (N2)

● With the help of children make a number frieze with a Spring theme: one blossom tree, two lambs, three baby rabbits, four eggs in a nest, five ducklings on a pond etc. On each picture display clearly the corresponding numeral. (N3)

Knowledge and Understanding of the World

● Choose a fine day to go for a Spring walk. Look for signs of Spring such as nests, leaves emerging from the earth, buds on twigs and minibeasts. Once back inside encourage children to describe what they saw and to record their observations in drawings and paintings. (K1, 2, 3)

● Use bulbs planted the previous term to show children how bulbs shoot and grow into plants. Explain that you are going to look at the plants each day. Make a timeline for the bulbs. Begin with a large display showing a plant pot and green shoots cut from sugar paper. Each week add other pots which show how the shoots have grown and the leaves and flowers starting to appear. (K2, 3)

Physical Development

● Mime being a bulb changing during Spring. Encourage slow, controlled movement. (PD1)

● Choose a nice day to use outdoor toys that were put away for the winter. Afterwards, encourage children to talk about the experience. (PD2, 4)

- Encourage children to be hungry caterpillars searching for food as they crawl and slither through hoops and larger apparatus with holes. (PD1)

Creative Development

- Use buds found in pot-pourri to make collages of trees in blossom. Encourage children to look at real trees in blossom (or use pictures) and to describe the colours and scent. (C1)
- Observe real daffodils. Encourage children to look closely at them, to count petals and leaves and explain that they will be making accurate models of the daffodils. Use egg cartons or bun cases for the trumpet, yellow card petals, green card leaves and green straws. Write children's names on the leaves before arranging them in a large vase. (C1)

Activity: Being bulbs

Learning opportunity: Moving with control and imagination. Listening to instructions.

Early Learning Goal: Physical Development. Children should move with confidence, imagination and in safety.

Resources: *The Tiny Seed* by Eric Carle.

Organisation: Whole group in a large space.

Key vocabulary: Bulb, shoots, bud, flower.

What to do: Talk to children about Spring being a time of new life. Remind them of the signs of Spring they saw on their walk. Show children the pictures in the book for the part of the story relating to Spring and talk about what is happening.

Explain that the children are going to be bulbs, turning into shoots, growing buds and finally bursting into flower. Talk about the kinds of shapes children will need to make themselves into.

Ask children to be a bulb (tightly curled up), a shoot (long and thin), roots growing under ground (wriggle toes), in bud (clenched fist), in flower (open hands, tall and stretched). As children try each stage praise those who make controlled, clear shapes.

Talk to the children about how plants grow over time and that things happen gradually. Repeat the mime but this time tell the story of the bulb, encouraging children to listen to the details and to change gradually and smoothly.

Activity: Making nests

Learning opportunity: Recognising features of nests, selecting materials and building nests.

Early Learning Goal: Knowledge and Understanding. Children should find out about and identify some features of living things, objects and events they observe. They should build and construct with a wide range of objects, selecting appropriate resources and adapting their work where necessary.

Resources: Pictures of common birds and birds' nests; old nests; a range of materials for making nests including made and natural materials.

Organisation: Small group.

Key vocabulary: Twigs, grass, moss, nest, soft, safe, warm.

What to do: Show children either pictures of birds' nests or examples of old nests. Remind them that they should never touch or disturb a nest which is in use. Explain that the old ones are no longer used by the birds.

Talk about the types of birds that might have lived in the nests. Look closely at the nests, the materials they are made from and how they are made. If nests were seen on the Spring detecting walk, talk about them.

Show children a range of materials they might like to use to try making a nest. Encourage them to think about a particular bird. How big is it? Where might it build its nest? What materials would it use? Show children how twigs can be bent into a nest shape.

Ask the children to make a nest. If old nests or natural materials such as twigs and leaves are used remind children to wash their hands thoroughly after finishing the activity.

Display

Display the tree collages on a notice board. Place the nests on a table in front of the board. On another board begin the bulb timeline display described above. Place the vase of model daffodils and growing plants nearby. Begin a display of the books read during the week and the group's version of The Very Hungry Caterpillar. As the topic progresses invite children to find other books for each week's theme.

Planning
for Learning
through
The Seasons **11**

Week 2
Frogs

Personal, Social and Emotional Development

- Set up a tank with frog spawn in the room. Talk to children about where the spawn came from and how it will change. Explain that it will be returned to where it came from. Talk about how children should be 'gentle giants' when dealing with living creatures. (PS3, 10)

Communication, Language and Literacy

- As a group make a collection of words to describe frogspawn. Write them on circles of card. (L11)
- In small groups, talk about what it would be like to be a tadpole in the tank. What would they see? Make up a group story. (L7)
- As soon as the spawn has hatched into tadpoles ask the children to work in small groups to observe and describe the tadpoles. Cut out tadpole shapes of black paper and on these scribe, or help children to write their own, descriptive words in white crayon. Display the tadpoles on a large pond. (L7, 8)
- Cut out a card frog shape for each child and ask them to write their name or draw a picture of themselves onto it. Explain that the frog labels will be used to identify ponds they are going to make - see activity opposite. (L18)

Problem Solving, Reasoning and Numeracy

- Sing and act out 'Five Little Speckled Frogs' from *Apusskidu*. (N1, 2, 7)

Knowledge and Understanding of the World

- Observe frog spawn turning into tadpoles. Each child can record the process on card cut into the shape of a fish tank. For example, on day one they could stick on frog spawn made from bubble wrap or white circles with black dots. As changes are noted new spawn/tadpoles can be added to the tanks. NB It is best to return the tadpoles to their natural surroundings as soon as they have hatched. The development of legs and the change to frog can be discussed with the aid of good picture books such as Tadpole and Frog by Christine Back and Barrie Watts. (K2, 3)

Physical Development

- Talk about the way frogs jump. Show children how to jump like frogs. Tell a story about a frog on a Spring day. Include descriptions of how the frog jumps and where it goes. Encourage the children to pretend to be the frog in the story, acting out its adventures. (PD1)
- Use PE mats or chalked areas to play the lily pad game on a large scale - see activity opposite. Remind children how to land with bent knees when they jump. Encourage light movements and long/high jumps. (PD2)

Creative Development

- Make model ponds in shoe boxes - see activity opposite. (C3)

Activity: Lily pad game

Learning opportunity: Counting to ten.

Early Learning Goal: Problem Solving, Reasoning and Numeracy. Children shoudl say and use number names in order in familiar contexts. They should count reliably up to ten everyday objects.

Resources: 20 lily pads cut from green sugar paper or card; a bean bag frog or soft toy; a die; four different coloured counters cut from card in the shape of tadpoles.

Organisation: Group of four children on the floor or around a small table.

Key vocabulary: Numbers up to ten, start, finish, first, next.

What to do: Show children the lily pads. Together arrange the lily pads on a large piece of blue paper in a 'squiggly' line ending with one with the frog on it. Give each child a tadpole to place on the lily pad furthest from the frog.
In turn the children shake the die and move their tadpole towards the frog. The winner is the first one to land on the frog's pad.

Children must throw the exact number to win ie, if it is two spaces to the pad a three cannot be used. As children play, encourage them to count aloud and to count how many pads they still have to go on to finish.

Activity: Make a model pond

Learning opportunity: Children will work collaboratively to make model ponds.

Early Learning Goal: Children should explore... texture, shape, form and space in... three dimensions.

Resources: Cereal boxes; brown and green paints; coloured tissue papers; pipe cleaners; pasta shells; bubble wrap; glue.

Organisation: Small groups.

Key vocabulary: Fold, stick, glue, under/on/in (the water).

What to do: For each group, turn a cereal box inside out and refasten the seams with masking tape. Cut a large hole in the front of the box so that when it lays flat the upper surface is open.

Show children how to paint the outside of the box in browns and greens to look like the banks of a pond. Provide modelling materials such as brown and grey tissue to crumple to make pebbles for the bottom of the pond, green shredded paper to make pond weed, shiny coloured paper to cut out fish, bubble wrap for frog spawn, black pipe cleaners to model tadpoles and pasta shells for snails.

For a finishing touch cover the open top of the pond with clear cellophane so that paper lily pads can rest on the water surface.

Display

Place the tank of frog spawn and a simple picture book about frogs on a table covered with blue cloth or paper. On a notice board create a scene of a pond and lily pads. Display the black tadpoles with words to describe them on the pond scene.

Put a tray of scraps of paper near the pond picture and invite children over the week in spare moments to make other creatures and plants that might be seen in or near a pond. Let children choose where they wish to place their animal or plant and encourage them to say why. Arrange the children's model ponds nearby with their frog labels.

Week 3
Spring rain

Personal, Social and Emotional Development

- Use a picture of a rainy day or a poem to talk through feelings about rain. Talk about the kinds of clothes people wear in the rain and the need to wipe feet and remove outdoor clothing when coming inside. (PS10)
- Discuss ideas for keeping a teddy dry if it were to go outside in the rain. Encourage children to share ideas and to say why they think their solution will work - see activity opposite. (PS2)

Communication, Language and Literacy

- Prepare a large card cloud from which to hang card raindrops. Use a rain maker instrument to stimulate children to describe the sound of rain. Scribe the words on the raindrops. (L14)
- Enjoy sharing stories and poems about wet weather. (L3, 8)
- Make a group big book about things children like to do in the rain. Encourage each child to draw a picture of what they like to do when it is raining. Under each picture scribe a sentence such as 'When it is wet I like to.....' or 'In the rain I like to.....'. Help children to write, trace or copy their name on the page. When the book is made share it with the group. (L17, 18, 19)
- Sing 'I hear thunder'. (L8)

Problem Solving, Reasoning and Numeracy

- Use the opportunity of water play to develop vocabulary related to capacity: full, empty, half full or half empty, more or less. (N11)
- Begin to measure capacity by counting how many small containers can be filled from one large one. Encourage children to predict and then count. Use the reverse procedure of counting how many times a small container can be filled and the water poured into a larger one. (N4)

Knowledge and Understanding of the World

- Use sieves, funnels and pots with holes to explore rain making. Which makes the largest drops? Which sound like rain on a very wet day? (K4, 5)
- Make rainy day pictures by painting on wet paper. Talk about what happens to the paint. (K4, 5)
- Talk about puddles. Where do they go? Draw around a puddle with chalk and observe it later in the day/week. (K3, 4)

Physical Development

- Talk about the way raindrops run down window panes. Use runny paint to do a blow painting. Ensure each child has a new straw. Encourage blowing not sucking! Discuss what the pictures remind children of. Ask each child to give their picture a title and scribe this for them. (PD2)

Creative Development

- Use tapping and clapping sounds to simulate a gentle trickle of rain, building up to a big storm then turning into a bright and sunny Spring day. (C1, 3)
- Make up a rain dance. (C5)

Activity: Rainy clothes for teddy

Learning opportunity: Working as a group and independently, initiating ideas and solving problems.

Early Learning Goal: Personal and Social Development. Children should be confident to try new activities, inititate ideas and speak in a familiar group.

Resources: A teddy; a range of scraps of materials including ones which would be waterproof; examples of real rainwear; Teddy in the Rain poem; photocopied outlines of a teddy; pencils, crayons, felt pens.

Organisation: Whole group sitting comfortably on the floor.

Key vocabulary: Waterproof, umbrella, Wellington boots, raincoat, plastic, rubber.

What to do: Read the poem to the group.

Teddy in the Rain
Outside it is raining
Teddy wants to be there,
But to keep his fur dry,
Special clothes he must wear.

He likes to splash in puddles,
Feel the rain upon his face,
And if his friend comes as well,
They will hold a sploshing race!

Teddy loves to be outside,
On a wet and rainy day,
So please help him decide
What to wear for rainy play!

Talk about being outside in the rain. What kinds of clothes do children wear in the rain?

Invite one child to put on the rainwear clothes. Why are they good in the rain? From what sort of materials are they made? How do the materials look and feel? Show the teddy to the children. Ask what would happen to him if he went out in the rain. What would he need to wear to stay dry? Show children the scrap materials. Ask them to suggest which would be best for a raincoat.

Give each child one of the photocopied teddies. Invite them to design an outfit which would keep the teddy dry. Children could either do a collage with the scrap materials or they could colour with pens and crayons. At the end of the session ask some children to show their pictures to the group and to explain why they have chosen the clothes and materials.

Activity: Tapping rain

Learning opportunity: Working collaboratively to make a rain tape.

Early Learning Goal: Creative Development. Children should respond in a variety of ways to what they see, hear... touch and feel.

Organisation: Whole group sitting comfortably on the floor in a circle.

Key vocabulary: Pitter, patter, drip, drop, splish, splosh, splash.

What to do: Talk about the sound of rain. If you have a rain maker instrument, listen to the sound it makes as it is tipped.

Show children how they can tap two fingers of one hand gently against the palm of the other. What kind of rain does it sound like?

Explain that the group is going to try to make the sounds of rain by tapping with their fingers and by clapping. Explain that they must listen carefully and watch. Encourage them to tap gently, copying the sound of light rain, to tap progressively louder for heavier rain, to clap for a downpour and then become quieter until eventually the rain stops.

Repeat the performance and tape record the sounds. Play the tape back. Discuss whether it did sound like rain and whether the children might like to change any of the sounds.

Display

On a large piece of paper in the shape of an umbrella write out the 'Teddy in the Rain' poem. Display this with the children's teddy clothes designs. If there are too many designs to go on the display some could be placed in clear plastic wallets and put in a loose leaf file on a table by the board. Put the group's big book about the rain and the teddy on the table. Hang the cloud of rainy words near the board.

Week 4
Woolly week

Personal, Social and Emotional Development

● If possible arrange a visit to a farm which has new lambs. Talk about caring for living creatures. (PS9)

Communication, Language and Literacy

● Recite 'Little Bo Peep'. Talk about what it feels like to lose something which is precious. (L3, 7, 8)
● Draw attention to the rhymes in the poem. 'Peep' and 'sheep' both contain an 'ee' sound. Saying this sound makes us smile! Can the children think of any other words with this sound? Give clues: 'I saw a kitten the other day. It was fast asl........', or 'When it was rainy I stepped in a puddle which was very d...... '. (L9, 10)

Problem Solving, Reasoning and Numeracy

● Play a simple number matching game with card sheep and a die labelled 1,1,2,2,3,3. Children pick up some sheep - they can choose to take one, two or three sheep. They then throw the die. If the number is the same as the number of sheep they took, they keep them. If not, they return their sheep to the pile. The game continues until no sheep are left. (N1. 2. 3)
● Use the sheep counting rhyme - see activity opposite. (N2)

Knowledge and Understanding of the World

● Talk about where wool comes from. Compare sheep's wool with wool bought from a shop. (K2, 3)
● Reinforce descriptive vocabulary relating to wool: soft, fluffy and warm. A piece of wool can be long or short. Which piece of wool is the softest? Can children find anything else in the room which is fluffy? (K2, 3, 9)

Physical Development

● Use the context of sheep following each other to introduce a game of follow my leader. Encourage the leading sheep to use actions, clapping, skipping, hopping and steps of different sizes. Introduce simple obstacles, such as a hoop to climb through stepping stone mats, a skipping rope on the floor to walk along or a set of cones to weave between. (PD1, 2)

Creative Development

● Make paper plate wool weavings. (C3)
● Make sheep collages by sticking white cotton wool balls on to green paper. Use black felt pen to add feet and a head to the sheep. Encourage children to use scraps of materials/draw to add other signs of Spring. (C3, 5)

Activity: Sheep counting rhyme

Learning opportunity: Using a counting rhyme for 1 to 5.

Early Learning Goal: Problem Solving, Reasoning and Numeracy. Children should count reliably up to ten everyday objects.

Resources: None.

Organisation: Whole group sitting comfortably on the floor.

Key vocabulary: Numbers to five.

What to do: Talk to the children about shepherds. What do shepherds do? Talk about the importance of looking after sheep and of counting to check that none are lost. Pick five children and ask them to kneel on all fours pretending to be sheep. Walk around the sheep saying the following rhyme as you go:

A shepherd in his field one day,
Finds a sheep sitting in his way
He pats the sheep saying 'Come with me,
(Pat one sheep)
One sheep and I will go home for tea.'

The child who is patted wakes up and follows you Repeat the rhyme changing the last line to two, three, ... until all the sheep have gone home for tea.

As you demonstrate the rhyme encourage the children who are watching to join in with the words and to clap their hands on the word 'pats'. Once the children know what to do, a child can be the shepherd.

Activity: Paper plate weaving

Learning opportunity: Exploring colour and materials.

Early Learning Goal: Creative Development. Children should explore colour, shape, form and space in two or three dimensions.

Resources: Small paper plates or card circles, notched around the edge using pinking shears. Wools in a wide variety of Spring colours.

Organisation: Small group with adult supervision.

What to do: Talk to the children about the colours which are associated with Spring. Talk about the colours of blossom, Spring flowers and so on.

Explain to the children that they are going to make some wool weavings to show these Spring colours. Encourage each child to select the colours of wools which they would like to include in their weaving.

Help each child to start weaving by taping the end of a long piece of their chosen wool to the back of their plate. Show how to wind the wool across the plate, catching it in the notches, so that the child ends up with something rather like the spokes of a bicycle wheel. Accuracy is not important. Now new colours and textures of wool can be woven between these spokes. Some children may enjoy weaving very carefully, but most will use the frame to hold pieces of wool in a fairly random manner. It does not matter. If the wools are thick and bright or fluffy all the results will be attractive.

As the children work, talk about the choices they are making. What does this colour remind you of? Does this wool feel quite the same as that one? Which wool is softer?

Encourage children to experiment with a variety of shades and textures. Some children may like to stick small twigs or coloured feathers into their pictures. Once mounted they can be used as the basis of Mothers' Day or Easter cards or just simply be appreciated as pictures of Spring.

Display

Make a display of children's clothes which are made from wool, balls of knitting wool, and books and pictures relating to sheep. Add captions which reinforce the processes involved in making woollen garments.

Week 5
Mother's Day

The topic of Mothers' Day should be dealt with sensitively so that no child feels excluded, whatever their personal circumstances. Mothers' Day should be viewed as an occasion when some people like to say thank you to their mother but others may prefer to focus on someone else.

Personal, Social and Emotional Development
- Use the 'Mother bakes' story opposite to discuss how 'little things matter'. (PS2, 5)
- Read *Five Minutes' Peace* by Jill Murphy. Talk about the mother elephant. How could the children have been more helpful? Discuss the ways in which children can help their parents. (PS4, 5)

Communication, Language and Literacy
- Help children to write a simple greeting and their name in a Mothers' Day card. (L17, 18, 19)
- Talk to the children about all the different jobs which mums do.
- Encourage each child to paint a picture of their own mum busy doing one of these things. Perhaps there is something special which their Mum is interested in or is especially good at. Talk to the children about their pictures and scribe captions using the children's own words at the bottom of each. (L13)

Problem Solving, Reasoning and Numeracy
- Use plastic animal families to practise sorting and grouping. Encourage the children to identify which animals they think are parents and young. How did they make their choices? (N4, 9)
- As the children play with the animals encourage their use as a context for counting and problem solving. 'How many ducklings are following the mother duck?' 'How many lambs does each mother sheep have? How many is that all together?' (N1, 2, 4)

Knowledge and Understanding of the World
- Talk about animal families, introducing and reinforcing the names of parents and young: a baby cat is a kitten, a baby horse is a foal and so on. Introduce some of the more specific names for male and female animals, such as cow and bull, mare and stallion. Reinforce the language by making a simple matching or happy families game. (K2)
- Invite a parent or friend with a young baby to visit the group. How does the baby need to be looked after? What can the children do that the baby cannot? (K3)

Physical Development
- Hold a Mum's Choice Day. Invite mums, friends and carers to show the children some of the games which they enjoyed playing when they were young. Examples might be ring games such as 'The Farmer's in the Den', 'The Hokey Cokey', 'Oranges and Lemons', or simple playground games such as Grandmother's Footsteps. (PD1)

Creative Development
- Make a mug-shaped card for a Mothers' Day card - see activity below. (C3)

Activity: Mother bakes

Learning opportunity: Working collaboratively. Initiating ideas.

Early Learning Goal: Personal and Social Development. Children should be confident to try new activities, initiate ideas and speak in a familiar group/ They should have a developing awareness of their own needs, views and feelings, and be sensitive to the needs, views and feelings of others.

Organisation: Whole group sitting comfortably on the floor.

What to do: Explain that the group is going to mime to a story about a mother who decides to bake a tart. As you tell the story mime the baking, reading and so on. Encourage children to join in.

Mum finds a bowl, some flour, some water, some salt and some fat. She mixes them together to make pastry. She rolls out the pastry, puts it in a pie dish, trims the edges, peels some apples and puts them in the dish. She covers it with more pastry, cuts it, pinches the edges and pops it in the oven.

While waiting for it to cook she reads a book. Suddenly she realises something smells nice. She puts on oven gloves and carefully takes the pie out. She cuts a slice, blows on it, and tastes. She shudders. It tastes horrible. She has forgotten to put the sugar on. It is sour!

The story is then repeated two more times. The second time she puts too much sugar on, the final time it is just right. She eats a slice, then another and so on until the pie has all gone, she feels full and falls asleep.

After the story talk to children about why only one pie tasted nice. Talk about the way just a small amount of sugar could make such a difference. Talk about little things children can do to make a difference such as picking up litter, saying 'please' and 'thank-you'.

Activity: Mothers' Day 'Have a tea break' cards

Learning opportunity: Exploring colour.

Early Learning Goal: Creative Development. Children should explore colour,... shape and space in two... dimensions.

Resources: Crayons, pens and for each child a pre-cut mug-shaped card (see below) and a fruit tea-bag.

Organisation: Small group.

Key vocabulary: The names of colours, extending to include 'bright', 'dark', 'pastel' and 'deep'.

What to do: Show children the mug card and how a fruit tea-bag string can be inserted through a slit in the card. Explain that each child can make one to send to a mother, friend or relation. Show children a variety of flavours of fruit tea-bags and encourage them to describe their scents. Which one would the person who will receive the card prefer?

Provide each child with a mug card and ask them to decorate it. Encourage children to think about the person for whom they are making the card. What colours and patterns would they like? When it's completed each child can select a tea-bag for their card.

Display
Mount and display the children's paintings of their mums to make a small exhibition. How many mums recognise themselves?

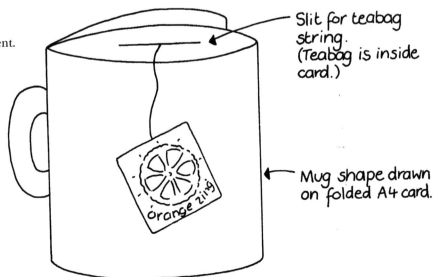

Slit for teabag string. (Teabag is inside card.)

Mug shape drawn on folded A4 card.

orange zing

Week 6
Spring parade

Personal, Social and Emotional Development

- Explain to the children that they are going to invite friends, parents and carers to visit their group to see some of the work they have been doing during the last few weeks. Use the opportunity to recap some of the key experiences of the topic, reinforcing relevant vocabulary. Invite the children to identify personal highlights. (PS2, 8)

Communication, Language and Literacy

- Involve the children in making invitations for the Spring parade. Encourage them to design and make their own cards but have ready-made photocopied 'inserts' giving relevant information, which can be glued inside each decorated card. (L1, 17)
- Work with the children to tell a collaborative, imaginative story. Begin with the discovery on the doorstep of a strange and wonderful egg. What do the children think it looked like? As you tell the story incorporate incidents which involve actions typical of individual children. Perhaps Amy took the egg to play with in the home corner, or Benji tried to play football with it. Stop at intervals to allow the children opportunity to contribute ideas and enjoy deciding together what will hatch out of the egg and the adventures to be had. Once started, you will find that the children will want to continue the story over several days. (L7, 8)

Problem Solving, Reasoning and Numeracy

- Prepare large, card egg shapes for children to decorate with bands of patterns. Provide printing blocks or pre-cut shapes to encourage the use of repeating patterns. Talk to the children about thepatterns they are making, the names of particular shapes, and the sequences being chosen. Which shape will come next? (N10, 11)

Knowledge and Understanding of the World

- Make and grow cress Spring bonnets - see activity opposite. (K3, 6)
- Uses a non-fiction book about animals to discover which ones hatch eggs. Play a game in which you repeatedly find an egg. Give the children clues and allow them to guess what sort of animals will hatch

from it. Encourage the children to suggest actions to represent the movements and sounds of the baby animal. (K2)

Physical Development

- Make musical egg shakers - see activity opposite. (PD8)

Creative Development

- Make Spring bonnets, hats or headbands.
- Use paper plates to form the basis of bonnets, with doilies or tissue paper flowers added and ribbons to tie. (C2, 3, 5)
- Make simple animal headband disguises by adding paper ears. (C2)
- Use grass made by fringing green paper to cover a headband and add spring animals, eggs or flowers. (C2)

Activity: Cress Spring bonnets

Learning opportunity: Selecting and cutting coloured paper. Observing cress seeds.

Early Learning Goal: Knowledge and Understanding of the World. Children should look closely at similarities, differences, patterns and change. They should select the tools and techniques they need to shape, assemble and join materials they are using.

Resources: Scissors, scraps of coloured papers, kitchen towel, cress seed, grown cress, double sided sticky tape and for each child a plastic tub inside a card bonnet as shown.

Organisation: Small group.

Key vocabulary: Sow, seed, shoot, grow.

What to do: Show children the card bonnets. Explain that they are each going to make a Spring bonnet in which to grow cress. Talk about how they might like to decorate their bonnet. Look at the papers. Which colours will they choose? Encourage children to decorate the bonnet sides and brim.

Show children some cress seed and a pot of grown cress. Ask them to describe what they see. Show them how to line the base of a pot with damp kitchen towel and how to sow cress seed thinly on the surface. Explain that each day children will need to look at their pot and to check the paper is still damp. Place the pots inside the bonnets and put them in a dark cupboard or cover them with a sheet of paper.

During the next few days children should be encouraged to observe the changes as the seeds swell and shoot. Once they have begun to shoot they should be placed in a light area.

NB It is best to do this activity at the start of a week so that the cress has time to shoot. The pots dry out quickly and should be taken home at the weekend.

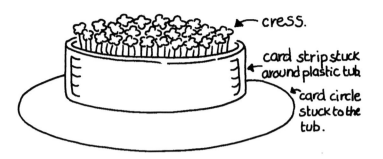

cress.

card strip stuck around plastic tub

card circle stuck to the tub.

how different instruments make slightly different sounds. Why do the children think this is so? Could it be that they have different things inside?

Explain to the children that they are going to make some shaker instruments of their own. Draw their attention to the plastic egg shapes, explaining that sadly they are empty! However, they are ideal for making small shakers which are easy for small hands to hold.

Talk to the children about the filling materials you have available and allow them to feel and handle them. Encourage each child to choose a filling for their personal shaker.

Show the children how to place a teaspoon of a chosen filling in one half of their shaker and then to fit the lid. These are often quite stiff and children will need adult help.

Encourage the children to then try out their shakers and to listen carefully to the sounds they can make. Do all the shakers make the same sound?

Suggest ways of decorating the outsides of the egg shakers.

Finally encourage children to shake the eggs rhythmically, perhaps adding stepping, foot tapping or singing or use them as an accompaniment to a nursery rhyme.

Activity: Musical egg shakers

Learning opportunity: Children use materials to make musical instruments.

Early Learning Goal: Physical Development. Children should handle... objects... with increasing control.

Resources: A collection of the small plastic containers found in some children's chocolate eggs which contain small toys. Various materials to use as fillings (rice, dried peas, sand) in pots, with teaspoons for handling. Sequins; glitter; glitter glue pens or gummed shapes to decorate. A small selection of shaker instruments.

Organisation: Small groups.

Key vocabulary: Shake, rattle, beat, rhythm.

What to do: Show the children the shaker instruments with which they are already familiar. (You may even have some commercially produced shaking eggs.) Talk about

Display

Hang the completed bonnets around one of the seasonal displays. This provides a safe storage space and adds an attractive border to the existing work.

Bringing It All Together

Introducing the Spring Parade

Talk to the children about the idea of a Spring parade. This will be a simple event, possibly occupying the last half hour of a morning session, to which parents, carers and friends can be invited. The children will show some of the work they have been doing and there will be a few activities with a spring theme for visitors to share. Discuss how the children might make preparations for welcoming visitors and entertaining them.

Involving the children in preparations

The introductory discussion will have helped children to understand that there are plenty of jobs to be done.

Food

Providing visitors with refreshments is not essential for a short event but it does present a purposeful context for children to develop simple culinary skills! Encourage the children to think about what sorts of food and drink might be appropriate. Ask them how they think the food should be presented. Decorate paper plates or paper tray covers in spring colours and patterns. (NB Care must be taken to avoid foods to which children may have allergies.)

Finger foods are easy for children to prepare:

- Use cress grown by the children to make cress, or egg and cress sandwiches.
- Preparing hard-boiled egg segments (perhaps served with a dip) gives an opportunity for children to observe changes caused by heat.
- Make Easter bonnet biscuits. Use icing as 'glue' to fix a large pink or white marshmallow sweet to the centre of a round biscuit. Drizzle icing over the 'brim' and decorate with tiny sweets or cake decorations.
- Make chocolate egg nests (see parent's page) to serve to guests.
- Allow children to make fruit cocktail drinks using a variety of juices with pieces of fruit to add panache! Encourage them to make decorated labels for the jugs, with pictures to represent the fruit juices used to make each drink.

Invitations

Encourage the children to think about the information that they need to provide for the people they are inviting.

You could collect children's ideas and make a photocopy of their suggestions to be pasted inside cards which children can decorate themselves. Alternatively highlight their ideas on a large sheet of paper which can be decorated by the children into a poster mural with Spring themes.

Activities

- Egg shell collage:
  Make hard-boiled eggs using water containing food colourings. You can use the eggs to make sandwiches, but use the coloured shell pieces as a collage material to cover prepared shapes. Make sure the children wash their hands after handling egg shells.
- Decorating eggs:
  Provide hard-boiled eggs and a variety of papers, felt pens, shiny scraps and glue to decorate. Cut lengths of card cylinders from the inside of kitchen roll to make 'collars' in which to display the finished eggs. If you have a marbling tray, adults and children will enjoy producing beautiful designs on real or card eggs. If real eggs are used they will need to be placed in a 'holder' for dipping. This can easily be made from a pipe cleaner looped and twisted around the egg, with a free end left for holding.
- Spring parade:
  Many young children would become distressed at the suggestion of a formal musical hat parade. However, they can enjoy wearing their creations during this event, and if materials are provided they will have the opportunity to help visitors to make similar models for themselves!

Songs:

A variety of Spring songs can be found in *Harlequin 44 Songs Round the Year* chosen by David Gadsby and Beatrice Harrop.

Resources

Resources to collect:
- A rainmaker - a colourful version can be bought from an Early Learning Centre shop.

Everyday resources:
- Boxes, large and small for modelling.
- Papers and cards of different weights, colours and textures - sugar, corrugated card, silver and shiny papers and so on.
- Dry powder paints for mixing and mixed paints for covering large areas such as card tree trunks.
- Different sized paint brushes from household brushes to thin brushes for delicate work and a variety of paint mixing containers.
- A variety of drawing and colouring pencils, crayons, pastels, charcoals, etc.
- Additional decorative and finishing materials such as sequins, foils, glitter, tinsel, shiny wool and threads, beads, pieces of textiles, parcel ribbon.
- Table covers.

Stories
- *Beaky* by Jez Alborough (Walker).
- *The Tiny Seed* by Eric Carle (Puffin Books).
- *The Very Hungry Caterpillar* by Eric Carle (Picture Puffins).
- *Hepzibah's Woolly Fleece* by Jill Dow (Frances Lincoln Ltd).
- *A Hard Day's Work* by Mick Gowar (Delacorte Press).
- *Alfie's Feet* by Shirley Hughes (Red Fox Picture Books).
- *Billy's Beetle* by Mick Inkpen (Hodder Children's Books).
- *Emma's Lamb* by Kim Lewis (Walker).
- *Floss* by Kim Lewis (Walker).
- *The Shepherd Boy* by Kim Lewis (Walker).
- *Five Minutes' Peace* by Jill Murphy (Walker).
- *Can I Keep It?* by Tony Ross (Andersen Press).

Poetry Books
- *This Little Puffin* by Elizabeth M. Matterson (Puffin).
- *Five Little Monkeys* by Zita Newcome (Walker Books).

Non-fiction
- *Tadpole and Frog* by Christine Back and Barrie Watts (A & C Black). Good for pictures.
- *The Egg* René Mettler (Moonlight Publishing).
- *Pond Life* by Barbara Taylor (Dorling Kindersley). Good for pictures.
- *Eyewitness: Pond and River* (Dorling Kindersley).

Information for Adults
- *Spring Tinderbox* compiled by Chris Deshpande and Julia Eccleshare (A & C Black).
- *The Early Years Foundation Stage: Setting the Standards for Learning, Development and Care for Children from Brith to Five* (Deparment for Children, Schools and Families).

Home links

The theme of Spring lends itself to useful links with children's homes and families. Through working together children and adults gain respect for each other and build comfortable and confident relationships.

Establishing Partnerships

- Keep parents informed about the topic of Spring, and the themes for each week. By understanding the work of the group, parents will enjoy the involvement of contributing ideas, time and resources.
- Photocopy the parent's page for each child to take home. This will give parents additional information which will enable them to support the topic through shared activities, encouraging children to be aware of seasonal changes in their environment.
- Invite friends, carers and families to attend the Spring parade.

Group Visitors

- In Mother's Day week, invite mums and carers to suggest favourite games for the children to play.
- During the same week, it is suggested that a mother and baby be invited to the group to talk about meeting a baby's needs.
- Invite keen gardeners to talk to the children about choosing and growing seeds.

Resource Requests

- Make a collection of the plastic egg-shaped containers from the insides of chocolate eggs. These are for making shakers.
- Additional plastic farm animals or pictures of farm animals will be useful.

Preparing the Spring Parade

- Help may be needed in supporting children as they make their spring bonnets. At the event it will be helpful to have additional adult helpers to assist children as they take charge of their games and stalls.

Parent's Page

We have been using the theme of Spring to introduce your child to different areas of learning. If you would like to follow this up at home, here are a few activities you might like to try. Play activities should be fun. Do not try to force your child to learn.

Talking

- Tell your child about the things you enjoyed doing in Spring as a child. Perhaps you were involved in May Day or Easter parades, or went egg rolling in the park. Show your child any photographs you may have kept. Encourage your child to see differences and similarities between the present and past. Have you retained any family customs?

Making

- Show your child how to make a simple rain gauge from a clear plastic bottle, as shown below. Help your child to measure and to record the rain over two weeks.
- Have a go at making Easter greetings cards together. The diagrams to the right show one idea you could try. The egg can be decorated with shiny scraps, coloured egg shell or colouring pens.

Story Telling

- Visit your local library with your child to look for books which feature Spring.
- All children love listening to stories. Make up a story about your child enjoying a Spring adventure. These are especially effective if continued from day to day. Encourage your child to join in, helping you to decide on the events for each exciting instalment.

In the Kitchen

- Make chocolate egg nests. Melt some chocolate in a dish placed over a bowl of hot water. Stir in cornflakes, rice krispies or crushed biscuits. Spoon the mixture into bun cases and decorate with an egg shaped sweet. As you bake, talk about the way the chocolate melts, the colours of the eggs and real birds' nests.

Out and About

- As you go for walks look for signs of Spring. Help children to notice buds and leaves. Encourage children to listen to the sounds of birds, to observe mini-beasts and insects and to notice the clothes people wear as the days grow warmer.

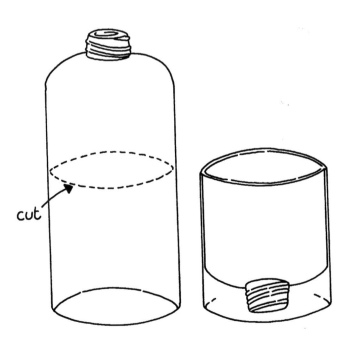

cut

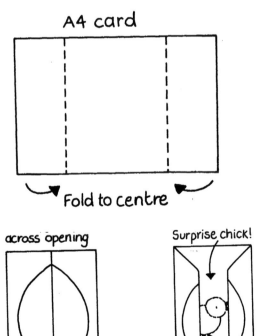

A4 card

Fold to centre

across opening

Surprise chick!

Egg

Skills overview of six-week plan for Spring

Week	Topic Focus	Personal, Social and Emotional Development	Communication, Language and Literacy	Problem Solving, Reasoning and Numeracy	Knowledge and Understanding of the World	Physical Development	Creative Development
1	Detecting spring	Appreciating the environment; Being sensitive to others	Talking; Listening; Role play	Counting; Number recognition	Observing; Recording; Identifying Features; Conditioning	Moving imaginatively; Increasing control	Handling materials
2	Frogs	Treating living things with care and concern	Listening; Writing; Talking	Counting	Comparing;	Jumping	Collaborative building
3	Spring rain	Problem solving; Sharing ideas	Discussing; Writing	Developing language; Measuring	Comparing; Observing	Handling materials with control	Composing music; Dancing
4	Woolly week	Treating living things with care and concern	Rhyming	Counting	Observing; Comparing	Moving with imagination and awareness of space	Working with a variety of materials
5	Mother's Day	Helping others; Discussing feelings	Discussing; Describing; Early writing	Sorting; Grouping; Problem solving	Language development; Comparing	Playing games collaboratively	Cutting and folding
6	Spring parade	Developing new ideas	Knowing that words and pictures carry meaning; Early writing	Recognising shapes; Patterns	Comparing; Observing; Questioning	Using materials with control; Moving with imagination	Folding; Cutting; Joining

Planning for Learning through The Seasons

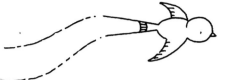

Summer

Topic Contents

Week 1
Detecting summer

Personal, Social and Emotional Development

● Go on a walk to detect signs of the summer. Before you go, talk about the importance of staying together, listening to instructions and being sensitive to the environment. (PS5, 8)

● Use a camera to record your walk. When the photographs are developed the children can work collaboratively to make a large book about the walk. (PS8)

Communication, Language and Literacy

● Encourage children to talk about the things they like to do in the summer. Look at pictures of people outside in the summer. Talk about the clothes people wear and what they are doing. (L1, 3, 8)

● Start to build a word bank of summer words. Scribe words suggested by the children on large pieces of card or stiff paper (for example, ice-cream, sun, hot, seaside). Ask children to draw pictures by the words to illustrate them. (L12, 17)

Problem Solving, Reasoning and Numeracy

● Make ladybirds by painting small pebbles or red plastic lids from plastic milk bottles. Vary the number of dots on the ladybirds from one to six. Play simple dice and estimation games (see activity opposite). (Nl, 2, 3)

● Show the children a large, safe thermometer, such as those from educational suppliers. Talk about how thermometers are used to measure how hot or cold something is. Introduce the word 'temperature'. Link to experiences children may have had in having their temperature taken. Show how the thermometer has numbers on it, and that the bigger the number is, the hotter the temperature. What is the temperature of the air in the room? (N3)

Knowledge and Understanding of the World

● Go on a minibeast hunt, encouraging children to look closely in small places, such as under a stone. Talk about why they need to be careful as they search. Explain that they are like giants in the world of tiny creatures and any disturbance, especially handling, should be avoided. (Kl, 2, 3)

● Begin a sunny day chart to talk about in Week 3. Ask children each day how hot or sunny it is. Record this with sunny faces. If it's very hot, use either more suns or vary the size of the sun. (K3)

Physical Development

● Make marble minibeasts and use them to go round card tracks (see activity opposite). (PD7, 8)

● Enjoy playing with bats and balls. (PD7)

Creative Development

● Encourage children to think about the sounds they hear during the summer: lawn mowers, ice-cream vans, insects buzzing, birds singing, sea sounds or perhaps even a thunderstorm. Recreate these sounds using percussion instruments and body sounds. (Cl, 3)

● Provide the children with large sheets of paper, brushes, paint or bright pastels and encourage them to make a picture of themselves carrying out a favourite summertime activity. (Cl, 2, 5)

Activity: Ladybird games

Learning opportunity: Counting to six.

Early Learning Goal: Problem Solving, Reasoning and Numeracy. Children will be able to recognise and use numbers to six.

Resources: 24 ladybirds made from red plastic milk bottle lids or painted pebbles (four ladybirds with one dot, four with two dots, and so on); four A4-sized leaves made from green felt; a dice numbered one to six; a dice numbered 0, 1, 1, 2, 2, 3.

Organisation: two to four children seated at a small table or comfortably on the floor.

Key vocabulary: How many . . .? Count, ladybird, leaf, one, two, three, four, five, six.

What to do: Show the children the ladybirds. Encourage them to work together to sort them into sets according to the number of spots. Ask children how many are in each set. Explain the rules and play one of the games below.

Give each child a leaf. Use the 0 to 3 dice. Check that children recognise and understand the numbers. In turn children shake the dice, pick up the number of ladybirds and place them on a leaf.

Give each child a leaf. Use the 1 to 6 dice. In turn children shake the dice and collect a ladybird with the same number of spots. The aim is to collect one for each number one to six. If children throw a number they have already collected they do not pick up a ladybird.

Put out six ladybirds. Ask children to count them. Spread them out. Ask how many there are. Count to show there are still six. Ask children to close their eyes. Take two of the ladybirds and hide them under a leaf. Ask the children to open their eyes and say how many are hiding. Help the children to count the four they can see and to work out that two are under the leaf. Repeat by hiding other numbers.

Activity: Marble minibeasts

Learning opportunity: Using scissors with control and regard for safety. Controlling speed and direction of marble minibeasts through a maze.

Early Learning Goal: Physical Development. Children will be able to handle small equipment and tools safely and with control.

Resources: A ready-made marble minibeast; for each child a plastic drinks bottle lid; a marble; a piece of card about 10 x 10cm; a pair of scissors; felt pens or crayons; double-sided sticky tape; a pre-drawn maze on stiff A4 card.

Organisation: Up to six children seated around a table.

Key vocabulary: Minibeast, names for minibeasts made by the children.

What to do: Let the children look at the ready-made minibeast. Show them how it is made and suggest they make their own. A minibeast is cut from card and stuck to the top of the lid with sticky tape. Place a marble under the lid and invite children to take their creatures for walks.

Introduce children to the mazes - a simple route drawn on card with a start and finish. Show how the minibeasts can be steered along the routes. Encourage children to persevere!

Display

Start a summer wall display by making a background of grassy green with occasional sponge printed leafy trees. As the topic progresses children will enjoy adding cut- outs of themselves carrying out various activities, or can add items which will personalise the display to your area. Examples might include a feature of a local park, familiar characters or buildings. Display the children's illustrations of summer activities, with suitable captions dictated by the children.

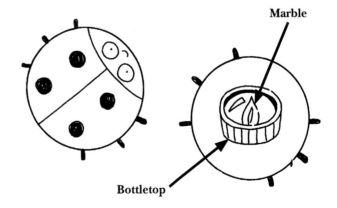

Minibeasts cut out of card and coloured with crayons

Underside of card ladybird

Marble

Bottletop

Week 2
Summer fruits

Personal, Social and Emotional Development

- Having first checked that no child has a fruit allergy, show children a bowl containing a selection of summer fruits. Talk about the types of fruits children like to eat and why. Explain that it is healthy to eat fruit. At snack time remind children to wash their hands and then eat pieces of apple. (PS1, 6, 11)
- Talk about the dangers of picking fruits without adult supervision. Even familiar fruits growing in gardens can hide hidden dangers, such as wasps later in the summer. (PS1, 9)

Communication, Language and Literacy

- Set up the role-play area as a fruit and flower market stall. Encourage children to take it in turns to be traders and customers and to talk about the reasons for buying the produce. (L7)
- Use the role-play area as the stimulus for children to make summer shopping lists in words and/or pictures. (L2, 3)
- Make a collection of words which can be used to describe fruits. Start by looking at the shape of the fruit. Talk about the colour and texture of the outside, and finally break or cut open the fruit to see the inside. Allow the children to touch and smell the fruit before dividing it into tiny pieces for tasting. (L5, 7)

Problem Solving, Reasoning and Numeracy

- Sort pips, fruits or pictures of fruits into sets by shape, type or colour. Use the same items to make sets of given numbers: 'Can you make sets of four?' (N2, 6)
- Use the banana finger rhyme (see activity opposite) or adapt familiar ones for the summer fruit theme. (N1, 2)
- As you carry out the fruit printing activity talk about halving the fruit or cutting it into quarters. As the children print encourage the use of repeating patterns. (N10)

Knowledge and Understanding of the World

- Use fruit purees sold as baby foods to carry out a 'taste and try' activity. Can children identify the

different fruit flavours? (Baby foods are amongst the safest possible to use for this type of activity but check group allergy records before any tasting activity.) (K1, 3)
- Make bookmarks from pressed flowers. (K1, 2, 3)

Physical Development

- With the children sitting in a circle, go around the group allocating the name of a fruit to each child. Use a repeating selection such as apple, pear, orange, lemon, apple ... so that there are several children in each fruit group. Explain to the children that you are going to make up a story, and that each time their fruit is mentioned they are going to do a particular action, for example, apples - clap, pears - stand up. Now make up a story, perhaps about a trip to a fruit market, and gradually speed up the frequency with which different fruits are mentioned! (PD2)
- Sing action rhymes with a fruit theme, such as 'Here is the tree with leaves so green' {This Little Puffin-see Resources, page 21). (PD1)

Creative Development

- Use pastels and chalks to make close observational pictures of fruits. Encourage children to match colours accurately. Provide each child with a piece of scrap paper for trying out colours. Show children how a small piece of sponge can be used to smudge chalks and pastels to mix the colours. (C2)
- Print with pieces of fruit (see activity opposite). (C3)

Activity: Fruit printing

Learning opportunity: Using a variety of materials for printing.

Early Learning Goal: Creative Development. Children will be able to explore texture, shape, form and space in two or three dimensions.

Resources: Safe fruit knife, cutting board, sugar paper, ready mixed or thick powder paints, saucers, sponges, variety of fruits such as lemon, apple, pear, orange, star fruit (avoid stoned or very soft fruits).

Organisation: Children working in a small group at a table. It is often more comfortable for small children to print from a standing position.

Key vocabulary: Names of fruits being used, colours of the fruits.

What to do: Give children a whole fruit to handle, reinforcing vocabulary which describes its colour, texture, shape. Ask the children to tell you what they think is inside the fruit. Remind them about fruits they

have eaten to help them. Cut through the fruit and compare with the children's ideas.

For each colour of paint you wish to use, prepare a sponge by covering it in paint and placing it in a saucer. Show the children how to press their cut fruit onto a sponge before pressing it onto their paper.

Demonstrate how to hold the fruit firmly and steadily to avoid a smudged print.

Talk about repeating patterns and designs. Would the print be the same if the fruit was cut in a different way?

Activity: The banana counting rhyme

Learning opportunity: Developing familiarity with numbers to five.

Early Learning Goal: Problem Solving, Reasoning and Numeracy. Children will be able to say and use number names in order in familiar contexts and count reliably everyday objects.

Resources: None.

Organisation: Whole group.

Key vocabulary: One, two, three, four, five.

What to do: Use carpet or circle time to learn and enjoy this rhyme. After each verse count the fingers being held up to reinforce number awareness.

Five bananas in a bunch
(*Hold up five fingers*)

I break one off to have for lunch.
(*Mime undoing the banana and biting*)

I eat up my banana, and I throw the skin away
(*Mime throwing skin in bin*)

Four bananas left for another sunny day.
(*Hold up four fingers*)

Last verse:
One banana from my bunch
I pick it up to have for lunch.................

Display

Display the fruit printing work with examples of the fruits used to make them. Can children or visitors tell which fruit was used to make each print?

Week 3
Summer flowers

Personal, Social and Emotional Development

- Talk about the occasions on which flowers are given as gifts. Show children how to make paper flowers which they can give to a chosen person as a thank-you. (PS5)
- Read the story "My naughty little sister is very sorry'" from *My Naughty Little Sister's Friends* (see Resources, page 21). Discuss the feelings of both the little sister and the neighbour from whose garden she picked the flower. (PS5, 9)

Communication, Language and Literacy

- Involve the children in making a flower alphabet display, using flower books and garden catalogues. (L10)
- Sing or recite nursery rhymes with a flower or plant theme; 'Lavender's Blue' 'Mary, Mary Quite Contrary' or 'I had a Little Nut Tree'. (L4, 6)
- Read the story of Titch (see Resources). Use the story to introduce and develop comparative language relating to size. (L4)

Problem Solving, Reasoning and Numeracy

- Use plant catalogues for children to make sets of flowers. For example, ask children to cut out three orange flowers, five pink flowers and one yellow. Stick the flowers in sets. Introduce early addition by asking more able children to count the flowers. (N2, 5, 6)
- Make daisy counting chains (see activity opposite). (N2)
- Cut out petal shapes in a variety of colours which children arrange around yellow flower centres. Introduce ideas of pattern as children place petals in alternate colours or make repeating patterns. Can the children recognise and continue a pattern which you begin? (N10)

Physical Development

- Draw a set of flower-shaped targets on the ground outside, using playground chalk. Alternatively draw them on the sides of large boxes which can be weighted to keep them stable. Use bean bags to practise throwing and aiming. (PD5)

- Play ring games with a flowery theme, such as 'Ring a ring o' roses', 'Here we go round the mulberry bush' and 'In and out the dusky bluebells'. (PD1)

Knowledge and Understanding of the World

- Talk to the children about the needs of growing plants. What happens to cut flowers if they are left out of water? Place some white flowers in a mixture of water and food colouring and leave overnight. What do the children notice? (K2,3, 9)
- Reinforce the names of the parts of a flower - petals, leaves and stem. Explain that although these can be different colours and shapes in different plants, the names of the parts stay the same. (K2, 3)
- Talk about the way in which plants are often grown in compost. Replace the sand in the sand tray with compost (bought from a garden centre rather than from your garden, though you can explain how compost can be made), and provide sieves, trowels and plastic plant pots as tools. Encourage the children to explore the texture and properties of the compost as they play. (Kl,3)
- Make pressed flower bookmarks (see activity opposite). (K2, 3)

Creative Development

- Use finger paints to make the petals and leaves in daisy pictures. (C3)
- Fold circles of tissue paper in half and then in half again. Using safe tapestry needles show the children how to thread these onto a length of shearing elastic, taking the needle through the point of the folded tissue each time. Once the threading is complete, tie the ends of the elastic together and open out all the folded tissue circles ; to make a flower garland, bracelet or anklet. (C2)
- Give each child a box with one face removed, to leave a tray-like container. Half fill with compost. Provide a selection of tiny twigs and flowers, such as daisies or buttercups, and let children create their own miniature gardens. Have modelling materials to hand as some children will enjoy making foil ponds, or lolly-stick fences. (C2)
- Use pasta to make a garden collage. To colour the pasta before use, place diluted food colouring in

a small bowl. Add a handful of raw pasta and mix. Drain, and spread the pasta on a baking sheet covered in non-stick parchment. Dry in a slightly warm oven. (Cl, 2)

Activity: Daisy chains

Learning opportunity: Using paper flowers as a context for counting.

Early Learning Goal: Problem Solving, Reasoning and Numeracy. Children will be able to count reliably up to ten everyday objects.

Resources: Prepared white daisy shapes, made by folding circles of white paper, cutting a petal outline and then opening out. Yellow or orange paper circles for the centres of the flowers. Strips of green paper, crepe paper or ribbon.

Organisation: Children working in small groups with an adult.

What to do: Show the children how to make white daisy flower shapes using the pre-cut shapes, and adding chosen centres.

Demonstrate how to glue the daisies to a strip of green paper, crepe or ribbon which can be hung vertically to make pretend daisy chains.

Count the daisies with the children and support the more able in writing an appropriate numeral in the centre of each flower to make a daisy counting line.

Activity: Pressed-flower bookmarks

Learning opportunity: Observing features of flowers.

Early Learning Goal: Knowledge and Understanding of the World. Children will be able to find out about and identify features of living things. They will look closely at similarities and differences.

Resources: PVA glue; stiff black card cut into bookmarks (about 21cm x 6cm); paper kitchen towel; sticky-back plastic; flowers to press; heavy books; a pre-made bookmark; a pen.

Organisation: Small group.

Key vocabulary: Five, flower, names of flowers used.

What to do: Show children the pre-made bookmark.

Explain that they are going to make one as a present for a member of their family (possibly for Father's Day). Show how flowers can be pressed by laying them in a piece of folded paper kitchen towel then placed in a heavy book. If possible, go to an area where children may pick flowers. Explain that flowers can only be picked where permission is given to do so.

Talk about the names of the plants and the colours. Ask children to pick five which look good together. Inside, help children to press their flowers. Write the child's name on the kitchen towel.

About a week later, remove the flowers from the books and help children to stick them with minimal glue on the black card. Once stuck an adult should cover the bookmark with clear sticky-back plastic or laminate it.

Display

Make a collection of household objects, fabrics or wrapping papers which have a floral design. Give the display a title such as 'Flowers all around us' and invite children to bring in objects (with parental permission) to contribute to the display.

Week 4
Sunny week

Personal, Social and Emotional Development

- Talk about sun safety. Show the children a selection of sun hats and sunscreen lotions. Make posters to encourage people to protect themselves from the sun. Encourage children to take responsibility for themselves by wearing hats and keeping in the shade. (PS4, 8)
- Talk about droughts and countries where it is always hot. Talk about ways we can save water such as not leaving the tap running when we clean our teeth. (PS5)

Communication, Language and Literacy

- Write a group poem about the sun. Display the poem in a big book. (L4, 18)
- Show pictures of children on a sunny day. Talk about the sequence of events as a child wakes and dresses on a sunny morning. (L7, 8, 12)
- Play a version of the 'I went shopping' game. Children sit in a circle. The first child starts the story by saying 'I woke up one sunny day and I . .' choosing a suitable activity with which to complete the sentence. The second child repeats the opening phrase and activity, and then adds their own. The game progresses around the group, each child adding their own activity to the list. Encourage all the children to help each other to remember the list in their turn. (L2, 3)

Problem Solving, Reasoning and Numeracy

- Make paper fans from concertina folded A4 paper. Colour the fan with repeating patterns. (N10)
- Talk about the sun making shadows and then play a shadow guessing game. You will need a collection of familiar objects, such as a teddy, a toy car, a fork or a cup. Make a simple screen from a large piece of white paper. Ask a child or adult helper to hold the screen slightly in front of you. Hold one of the objects between yourself and the screen. Using the other hand, shine a torch onto the object, casting a shadow onto the screen. Can the children guess the mystery objects from their shadows? (N11, 12)

Knowledge and Understanding of the World

- Talk about the differences between day time and night time. (Bear in mind that children who live in cities may have little experience of starry skies.) Introduce vocabulary such as morning, afternoon, evening, last night, yesterday. (K3)
- On a sunny day go outside to investigate shadows. Can the children escape from their shadows? Does it always copy movements exactly? Can the children jump over their shadows? (K2, 3, 4, 9)
- Allow the children to take objects outside to investigate shadows. Interesting shadow makers include objects with holes in them, such as sieves, colanders, or plant pots. How does the shadow change as the object is turned? (K2, 3, 4, 9)
- Make a suncatcher (see activity opposite). (K2, 4, 5)

Physical Development

- Remind the children about the importance of staying in the shade on a hot, sunny day. What types of activities do the children enjoy playing in the shade? Invite a parent or grandparent into the group who is able to demonstrate some of the playground games of skill which they enjoyed as children: marbles, jacks or tiddlywinks. (PD2, 5)
- Play musical shadows. Take a musical instrument outside and explain to the children that they are going to move around to the sound of the instrument. WT"ien the instrument stops, you will tell them what sort of shadow to make, for example a tall shadow, a small shadow, a spiky shadow or a wide shadow. (PD1, 2)

Creative Development

- Make a sunshine collage. Provide wool, paper scraps and curls, dyed pasta or woodshavings, fabric scraps and so on, all in bright reds, yellows and oranges. Stick them on to round shapes pre- cut from yellow paper or card. (C3)
- Cut out pictures from greetings cards and mount them on straws to make simple shadow puppets. Provide a screen to either take outside in the sunshine, or to use with a torch indoors. (C5)

Activity: Making a suncatcher

Learning opportunity: Exploring aspects of colour and transparency.

Early Learning Goal: Knowledge and Understanding of the World. Children will be able to find out about and identify features of objects.

Resources: Small boxes (mini cereal boxes), coloured cellophane, scissors, sticky tape or glue, string.

Organisation: Children working in small groups at a table.

Key vocabulary: Hole, the colours of the cellophane.

What to do: Help each child to cut out very large holes in the four sides of a small box. Leave the top and bottom intact.

Cover the holes with coloured cellophane. Encourage the use of a different colour in covering each hole. Accuracy is not crucial.

Finally, tape a length of string to the top of the box so that it can be hung in front of a window at child height.

As the box turns in the sunshine the children can spot the colours which they see. Sometimes a coloured pattern will be seen on a wall or the floor.

Activity: Write a sunny poem for a big book

Learning opportunity: Using descriptive words. Collaborating to make a big book.

Early Learning Goal: Communication, Language and Literacy. Children will be able to interact with others, negotiating plans and activities and taking turns in conversation. They will write their own names and begin to form simple sentences.

Resources: Suns cut from large paper; pencils and crayons; large picture or poster of people outside on a sunny day (see Resources).

Organisation: Whole group introduction, small groups of up to eight children for the writing and drawing.

What to do: Introduction: Show the group a large picture of people on a sunny day. Talk about the types of activities people are doing. What do children do when it is sunny? Show the group the cut-out suns. Explain that together they are going to make a book about what children do on sunny days. Break up into small groups, each with an adult.

Small group development: Play a game in which each child completes the sentence 'When it is sunny (child's name) likes to . . . ' Encourage children to use descriptive words, for example, 'When it is sunny Jonathan likes to sit in icy water in his paddling pool'. After each child has had a go, talk about the responses. Were any similar? Can one child recall another's sentence? Give each child a sun and ask them to draw a picture of what they do when it is sunny. For each child scribe their sentence or help themzto overwrite/underwrite/copy it. When all are finished, read the whole 'poem' back to the group.

When all small groups have finished their suns, mount them in a big book and ask children who are able to write their name on the cover. Display the book in the reading area for all to share and enjoy.

Instead of making a big book, pictures can be drawn on smaller suns cut from A4 card. The sentence can then be written on the back and the suns hung from the ceiling at a level where children can look at or read them.

Display

Make a display of the sunshine collages together with some items of hot weather wear, such as sunglasses, swimming clothes, beach towel and a sunshade. If you have made card suns, hang them above the display.

Week 5
Summer holidays

Personal, Social and Emotional Development

- Tell a story about a child who goes on a day visit and behaves badly. Perhaps in the end she could wake to find it was a dream which gives her the chance to behave perfectly on the real outing! Use the story as the basis for discussion about how to behave in new places and the importance staying with an adult. (PS3, 8, 9)
- Talk to the children about the need for occasional breaks from work. Even if it is only a quiet sit down, everyone needs some time off! Suggest that they might give their mums or dads a short break by helping with a household chore, or playing quietly while they have a chat. (PS5)

Communication, Language And Literacy

- Play a holiday guessing game. Say to the children, 'These are the things I am going to pack - Can you guess where I am going?' Make up some lists which are indicative of particular types of places: a swimsuit, sunglasses, large towel and sunshade, or a warm jacket, trousers, hat, gloves, boots and skis. Fantasy ideas might include: a space helmet and astronaut's suit, or a pirate's hat, map and spade. Allow children to join in by making their own lists for others to guess. (L2, 3, 11)
- Make a travel agent's role-play area. Provide a desk, telephone, paper and pencils, pretend tickets and leaflets. Ask for unwanted posters from travel agencies to go on the wall. Provide a role model by showing children how to browse through the leaflets and then book a holiday with the help of the agency assistant. How would you like to travel? For how long will you be away? (L2)
- Make postcards to send. Show the children a selection of holiday postcards. Draw attention to their features: a picture on one side, a space to write in, a space for an address and a space to stick a stamp. Provide children with postcard- sized pieces of card and see if they can design and make their own fantasy postcards. More able children may enjoy writing a simple message on the back and filling in their own addresses. (L11, 15, 17, 18)

Problem Solving, Reasoning and Numeracy

- Make a packing/number recognition game (see activity opposite). (Nl, 3)
- How quickly can you pack? Make a timing game using a collection of a few suitable clothes or pieces of holiday equipment and a suitcase. In turn, children estimate how long it is going to take them to pack the case and then test their predictions. Use non-standard measures of time. How many times could other children sing a nursery rhyme during the packing or how many bricks could they stack? Make up rules for the packing, such as only one item to be packed at a time to make the game last longer. (N4, 6, 9)

Knowledge and Understanding of the World

- Talk about all the different ways of travelling. Encourage children to describe their experiences of trains, buses, cars and perhaps planes or boats. Sing action songs to match each form of transport, such as 'Down at the station', 'The Wheels on the Bus', 'Aeroplanes, aeroplanes all in a row', 'Here is the sea, the wavy sea'. All these can be found in This Little Puffin (see Resources). (K9)
- Talk about places the children have visited. How were they different from their own familiar locality? Illustrate with postcards. (K9, 10)

Physical Development

- Mime the events associated with preparing for a journey (packing clothes, preparing a picnic), travelling and arriving. Encourage children to describe their imaginary destination. (PD1)
- Make an obstacle course with each item representing an event on a journey, rather along the lines of 'Going on a Bear Hunt'. For example, the children could travel through a tunnel (play tunnel), over a mountain (climbing obstacle), between the trees (cones) and over the stepping stones to cross the river (mats). (PD2, 3)

Creative Development

- Sit with children on a mat or carpet and explain to them that this is a magic carpet. It can take the children wherever they would like to go for a holiday. The places they choose could be places they know or exciting imaginary places such as a land of giants. Follow the children's ideas, talk them through the events happening as you take off on your great adventure. Closing eyes can help children to focus on imaginative thoughts. (C1)

● Make a model caravan (see activity below). (C2)

Activity: The suitcase game

Learning opportunity: Recognising and matching numbers.

Early Learning Goal: Problem Solving, Reasoning and Numeracy. Children will be able to count reliably up to ten everyday objects. They will recognise numbers one to nine.

Resources: Prepared boards and pieces, dice.

Organisation: Up to four children at a time, depending on resources.

Key vocabulary: Numbers one to ten.

What to do: Prepare a game board for each child. This will take the form of a suitcase outline drawn onto card. Within the suitcase outline are the silhouette shapes of a pair of sandals, a sun hat, a pair of sunglasses, a pair of shorts, a T-shirt and a beach towel.

These items are also prepared as individual playing pieces, ideally mounted on card and laminated. Try to ensure that each piece matches its outline on the suitcase game board. In addition each piece has a number on it.

Pair of sandals	1	Sun hat	2
Pair of sunglasses	3	Pair of shorts	4
T-shirt	5	Beach towel	6

Children collect the items in their cases by throwing the dice, counting the spots and collecting the piece with the appropriate number. If the game becomes slow to finish, encourage children to add to each other's boards as they win pieces they do not need themselves.

Activity: Making a caravan

Learning opportunity: Using a variety of materials within an imaginative context.

Early Learning Goal: Creative Development. Children will be able to express and communicate their ideas, thoughts and feelings using a widening range of materials.

Resources: Shoe boxes, recycled modelling materials, additional materials (such as pipe-cleaners, lolly-sticks and fabric scraps), pre-cut card wheels, paint, brushes, scissors, glue, adhesive tape.

Organisation: Small group.

Key vocabulary: Caravan, house, wheels.

What to do: Ask the children if any of them have ever been in a caravan. What is a caravan like? Most children will have some understanding of the idea of a 'house on wheels'. Explain that they are going to make their own model caravans.

Show children how to use a shoe box as the main part of their caravan.

Provide a large selection of materials, such as small pieces of fabric, pieces of foil, card, small boxes such as ' matchboxes. Inside the shoe box they can use any materials they like to make the beds, tables, curtains and windows.

Put the lids on the boxes and then the outside of the caravan can be painted. Finally, the cardboard wheels are glued into place.

Display

Display a collection of children's souvenirs of their holidays or days out.

Week 6
Sports day

Personal, Social and Emotional Development

- Read *The Sports Day* by Nick Butterworth and Mick Inkpen. Talk about sports days. Talk about races and what it feels like to win and to lose (see activity opposite). (PS5)
- Remind the children about sensible precautions to take in case the sports day is sunny. Discuss the importance of sun hats and creams, spending time in the shade and having plenty to drink. (PS3, 9)

Communication, Language and Literacy

- Read *Dogger* by Shirley Hughes (see Resources). Do any of the children have older brothers or sisters who have school sports days? Use the story to introduce some of the events which they might see at a sports day (L3, 4, 7).
- At your sports day, each child will receive a certificate to mark their taking part. Encourage each child to help in writing their name on a certificate and perhaps decorating it. (L1, 2, 19)
- Through discussion, discover the sports with which children are familiar. Record the names of the sports on a chart and encourage the children to mime each sport as it is listed. (L3, 17)

Problem Solving, Reasoning and Numeracy

- Use the context of sports to introduce and reinforce the comparative language of speed: fast, faster, fastest; slow, slower and slowest. Use these words as children move around the room: clap, shake, nod, jump or play instruments. (N6)
- Races provide the opportunity to introduce ordinal numbers: first, second, third and so on. Illustrate these by enacting a toys' sports day with the children. Who do the children think would come first, second and third in each race? Encourage children to predict places in the Great Toy Car Grand Prix. Award rosettes to the winners of the teddy bear's race! (N1)
- Practise speedy movements and further develop a sense of time using sand timer activities. Set a series of challenges: How many beads can you thread before the sand runs through? How many times can you bounce a ball and catch it? (N11)

Knowledge and Understanding of the World

- Talk about body parts and how joints move. Make card people with brass fasteners for arm and leg joints (see activity opposite). (K4)
- Encourage children to notice changes which happen in their bodies as they exercise. Encourage children to be aware of feeling hot and out of breath. Practise warming up, exercising and cooling down. (K3, 4)

Physical Development

- Practise some of the activities for the sports day (see page 20). (PD1, 2)
- Sing action songs which concentrate on body movements such as: 'If you're happy and you know it', 'One finger one thumb keep moving', 'Head, shoulders, knees and toes'. (PD2)

Creative Development

- With the children sitting in a large space, play a guessing game in which you describe actions, clothes or equipment needed to play a particular sport. Once the children have guessed the sport' they can begin to mime its actions. Give more clues until all the children are joining in. (C4)
- Encourage the children to help in decorating information posters about the sports day. (C5)
- Reinforce the language of speed through a blow-painting activity. Children start with a blob of runny paint placed on a paper using a dropper or teaspoon. They then blow the paint using a clean drinking straw. The straw should be held low down, almost parallel to the paper in order to blow the paint effectively. Use phrases such as 'The paint is going really fast now. It's slowing down. It's stopped.' (Cl)

Activity: Sports day

Learning opportunity: Discussing how it feels to win and to lose and the importance of always trying to do your best.

Early Learning Goal: Personal, Social and Emotional Development. Children will have a developing awareness of their own needs, views and feelings and be sensitive to the needs, views and feelings of others.

Resources: *The Sports Day* by Nick Butterworth and Mick Inkpen; flip chart.

Organisation: Whole group.

Key vocabulary: Race, sports day, win, lose.

What to do: Read *The Sports Day*, or a similar story about a sports day. Talk about the types of races and how the children in the book might have felt when they did well and when things did not go quite right.

Discuss how in races it does not matter if you come first or last, what is important is doing your best. Also talk about how to react if you play a game and win. Talk about being sensitive to others feelings.

Explain that they are going to have a sports day. Tell them there will be lots of races and games. Some will be like the ones in the story but others might be games the children have played during the year. Ask children to suggest games and races that they would like to do and to say why they think they would be good. Encourage children to talk about some stationary games (How many toy bricks can you stack with one hand in a given time?) as well as the more active races which involve running. Record suggestions on a flip chart.

Activity: Card people

Learning opportunity: Asking questions about body joints. Using brass fasteners to join pieces of card together.

Early Learning Goal: Knowledge and Understanding of the World. Children will be able to ask questions about how things work.

Resources: Display board with background as a playing field; an example of a completed body. For each child: pre-drawn body parts on card (see illustration); colouring pens and crayons; scissors; four brass fasteners.

Organisation: Whole group introduction, six children for making the bodies.

Key vocabulary: Elbow, shoulder, knee, hip, bend.

What to do: Whole group introduction: Ask for a volunteer to stand up. Point to the child's elbows, shoulders, knees and hips. Check that children know the names for these joints. Ask children why it is useful to have knees which bend. Talk about things we can do because they bend (kick a ball, sit cross-legged). Ask a child to walk round the room without bending their knees. How easy was it? Talk about other joints of the body which help us to move. Show the children the jointed card person. Explain that they are each going to make one to look like a child on sports day. Talk about the kind of clothes it should wear. Show children how brass fasteners can be used for shoulder, elbow, knee and hip joints.

Small group: Ask children to colour the body parts and to cut them out. Attach the arms and legs with brass fasteners.

Display

Children can place their completed sports person on the playing field display. Fasten the person to the board using staples through the neck and bottom thus allowing children to alter the positions of the arms and legs.

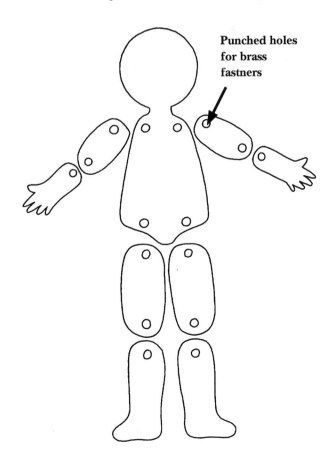

Punched holes for brass fastners

Bringing It All Together

Introducing the Sports Day idea

Explain to the children that in a few days time the group is going to hold a sports day. Remind the children of the work they have already done about sports days, and encourage them to contribute their ideas about what such an event might involve.

Explain to the children that on their sports day, everyone is going to have a go at several activities, and everyone is going to be a winner!

During the sports day the children move around a circuit of small activities. Each one is a challenge of skill.

Suggested ideas include:

- The rope maze Fold a very long skipping rope or washing line in half and lay it on the ground in such a way as to make a track which can be followed by children. Older children could be asked to roll a ball along the maze.
- The balancing rope This activity again starts with a rope laid on the ground, but this rope is used to form a single straight line. The children's challenge is to walk along the rope with feet at all dmes touching the rope. The skill is to keep the feet straight in front of each other, in what is essentially a balancing activity.
- Target throwing Make a simple target throwing challenge, such as throwing a bean bag into a bucket from a short distance.
- The obstacle course Make a mini obstacle course including, for example, hoops to climb through, stepping stones to cross, a held rope to crawl under and a plank on the ground to walk along.
- Skittles Use bought skittles, or make your own using washing-up liquid or plastic soft drinks bottles which can be decorated and slightly weighted.
- The ball rolling slalom Make a short slalom course by placing half a dozen cones in a spaced row. Children roll the ball in and out of the cones. This can be adapted as a steering activity if your group has ride-on toys.

Each activity will need to be manned by an adult (two in some cases). Children move around the activities in small groups, with a signal to move on given every few minutes. Each child taking part will need a prepared card with the name of each activity on it. As each activity is completed the card is ticked by the attending adult. Ensure that all supporting adults understand that this is not a competition for young children. Every child should receive as much support as they need to complete each station, including a little rule bending where necessary! Completion of the card earns a certificate, sticker, home-made rosette or tiny prize. (It is anticipated that every child with achieve this).

At this event there is unlikely to be any need for refreshment other than drinks and perhaps some biscuits. Some groups, however, may like to combine the event with a lunch or tea-time picnic, particularly if the weather is warm and sunny.

Preparations

Invite children to make suggestions about the types of activity which you might incorporate into your sports day event. Perhaps they have favourite activities they would like to include.

- Invitations Adult help will be vital to the success of this event. Support will be needed in looking after each event, serving refreshments and helping children to complete the challenges. Ask for help in a prepared letter which can be photocopied for parents and carers and pasted inside a piece of folded card. Involve children by asking them to decorate the outside of the cards. (Use the letter to remind parents and carers about the possible need for sun protection.)
  Children may like to invite younger brothers and sisters to join in the activities, or friends who do not normally attend the group. If so you will need to know numbers in advance so that enough recording passports and completion awards are available.
- Accessories Involve the children in: choosing refreshment drinks; writing their names on and decorating their personal recording passports which they will take with them around the events; making flags or signs to name each activity station.

Resources

Resources to collect:
- A few magazines, colour supplements and travel brochures.
- Shopping catalogues with pictures of summer clothes and outdoor toys.
- Examples of summer fruits, vegetables and flowers.
- Fruit juices for making iced lollies - arrange for access to a freezer if necessary.
- Small hand-held puzzles.
- Sea shells and small, clean pebbles.
- Seasonal posters and pictures such as the Practical Pre-school Seasons Posters - Spring, Summer, Autumn, Winter.
- A large, safe thermometer from an educational supplier.

Everyday resources:
- Boxes, large and small for modelling including shoe boxes and miniature cereal boxes.
- Papers and cards of different weights, colours and textures such as sugar paper, corrugated card, silver and shiny papers.
- Selection of coloured cellophane or acetates.
- Different sized paint brushes from household brushes to thin brushes for delicate work and a variety of paint mixing containers.
- A variety of drawing and colouring pencils, crayons, pastels, charcoals, chalks.
- Small yoghurt or fromage frais pots and lolly sticks.
- Table covers.
- Sand timers.

Stories
- *The Sports Day* by Nick Butterworth and Mick Inkpen (Hodder Children's Books).
- *Maisy Goes Swimming* by Lucy Cousins (Walker).
- *Oliver's Fruit Salad* by Vivian French (Hodder Children's Books).
- *Dogger* by Shirley Hughes (Walker).
- *Lucy and Tom at the Seaside* by Shirley Hughes (Puffin).
- *Titch* by Pat Hutchins (Red Fox).
- *The Giant Jam Sandwich* by John Vernon Lord (Pan Books).
- *My Naughty Little Sister's Friends* by Dorothy Edwards (Methuen/Magnet paperbacks).

Poems
- *This Little Puffin* by Elizabeth Matterson (Puffin).
- *Out and About* by Shirley Hughes (Walker).
- *Playtime Rhymes* by Sally Gardner (Orion Children's Books).

Information for Adults
- *The Early Years Foundation Stage: Setting the Standards for Learning, Development and Care for Children from Brith to Five* (Deparment for Children, Schools and Families).
- *Encouraging Early Sports Skills* by Sandy and Jake Green (Practical Pre-School Books)0

Home links

The theme of Summer lends itself to useful links with children's homes and families. Through working together children and adults gain respect for each other and build comfortable and confident relationships.

Establishing partnerships

- Keep parents informed about the topic of Summer, and the themes for each week. By understanding the work of the group, parents will enjoy the involvement of contributing ideas, time and resources.
- Request parental permission before taking children out of the group on a summer walk. Describe your route and the purposes of the activity. Additional parental help will be necessary for this activity to be carried out safely.
- Photocopy the parent's page for each child to take home.
- Invite friends, childminders and families to share the sports day.

Visiting enthusiasts

- Invite adults from other cultures to show children how some of the less familiar fruits and vegetables are used in traditional recipes.
- Sporting enthusiasts may be willing to come into the group to talk about their interests.

Resource requests

- Encourage contributions of summer finds from family walks.
- Ask to borrow summer coloured fabrics or seasonal pictures which could be used for displays.

Preparing for Sports Day

- Request adult help in making any small prizes, such as ribbon rosettes which are to be awarded at the sports day event.

Parent's Page

We are using the theme of Summer to introduce your child to different areas of learning. If you would like to follow this up at home with some fun activities here are a few ideas to try!

Talking

- Tell your child about the things you enjoyed as a child in summer. Perhaps you enjoyed bathing in the sea, going camping or picking strawberries.
- Talk about the importance of not picking any of the summer fruits which children see in hedgerows unless an adult has said it is safe to do so.

Making

- Make a set of wind chimes to listen to on summer days. Choose a set of objects which will make a sound as they rattle together - old metal or wooden spoons, tiny plant pots, threaded shells, short lengths of bamboo garden cane or even old pencils. Hang the objects to a branch using strong thread. They will need to be fairly close together if they are to act as chimes.
- If it is not possible to use a branch, fix two short pieces of stick or dowel together in a cross shape. Hang the objects from this and suspend it by an open window.

In the kitchen

- Ice lollies can be easily made in small yoghurt or fromage frais pots.
- Fill the pot about three quarters full with fruit juice. Cut a card circle which is just large enough to cover the pot. Make a slit in the circle and push a lolly stick through it. Once the fruit juice is frozen the card can be removed from the lolly-stick

Story telling

- Visit your local library with your child to look at books which feature summer.
- Make up a story about a magical summer journey dertaken by a favourite toy. Describe how the journey begins, the adventures the toy has in the magical places it visits, and the return home.
- As you walk or drive with children draw their attention to seasonal changes. Point out summery shop window displays, tourists in the cities and the appearance of summer gardens.
- Look for different shadows: those made by yourselves, and those made by trees, railings or

buildings. making strange shadow shapes together. Can you make a giant with two heads and four arms?

Packing practice

- If you are going on holiday, encourage your child to pack a small suitcase for a favourite toy. This will help to develop skills of organisation. Allowing your child to help with their own packing gives an opportunity to practise planning ahead, thinking about needs and folding clothes!

What will children have the opportunity to learn

- to experience handling different materials;
- to make up stories and use their imagination;
- to recognise seasonal changes;
- to ask questions, investigate and explore.

Skills overview of six-week plan for Summer

Week	Topic Focus	Personal, Social and Emotional Development	Communication, Language and Literacy	Problem Solving, Reasoning and Numeracy	Knowledge and Understanding of the World	Physical Development	Creative Development
1	Detecting summer	Sharing; Playing collaboratively; Being sensitive to others	Talking; Writing; Describing	Estimating; Measuring; Recognising number	Investigating; Recording	Fine motor skills; Moving with control	Making sounds; Listening; Painting
2	Summer fruits	Being aware of health and safety	Role-play; Describing	Sorting; Exploring pattern; Counting	Comparing; Using materials	Moving with control; Moving imaginatively	Using different media; Printing
3	Summer flowers	Discussing feelings; Appreciation of the environment	Comparing; Rhyming; Recognising letters	Comparing; Sorting; Counting; Repeating patterns	Investigating; Observing	Aiming; Throwing; Playing collaboratively	Finger painting; Sewing; Modelling
4	Sunny week	Awareness of safety; Care of others	Sequencing; Telling stories	Repeating patterns; Matching shape; Awareness of time	Observing; Investigating; Using materials	Fine motor skills; Moving with imagination and awareness of space	Gluing; Using materials
5	Summer holidays	Sharing; Discussing feelings and behaviour	Role-play; Describing; Early writing	Measuring time; Recognising numbers	Describing; Comparing	Using large apparatus; Moving with awareness of space	Role-play; Modelling
6	Sports Day	Discussing feelings	Writing names; Early writing; Discussing	Ordinal numbers; Comparing	Naming body parts; Observing changes	Gross fine motor skills; Moving with imagination	Miming; Blow painting

Planning for Learning through The Seasons

AUTUMN

Topic Contents

Week 1
Detecting Autumn

Personal, Social and Emotional Development

- Encourage children to care for their environment. Discuss the need to be 'gentle giants' and not tread on minibeasts, to take care of plants and to leave places we visit as we would wish to find them. When on a walk, look out for areas where we need to take care. If appropriate, talk about the country code. (PS4,9)
- Work collaboratively to make an Autumn display of items collected on the Autumn walk and paintings of signs of Autumn. (PS2 ,8)

Communication, Language and Literacy

- Talk about changes the children saw on their walk which describe Autumn. Encourage children to use descriptive vocabulary for their observations. (L12)
- Show children pictures of a scene in Summer and Autumn. Ask children to compare trees, weather, people's clothes and so on. How many changes can the children spot? (L2)
- Read an Autumn poem such as 'Misty' in *Out and About* by Shirley Hughes (Walker Books). Use this as the stimulus to write a group poem beginning with the words 'Autumn is.....'. Scribe the children's ideas on separate large pieces of paper. Ask children to illustrate their 'line' and make a big book poem. If appropriate ask children to write their names on the book cover. (L4, 12, 15, 18)

Problem Solving, Reasoning and Numeracy

- Make a pelmanism-type game in which children can match the numbers of autumn leaves, squirrels, acorns and conkers. Use numbers up to five. Encourage children to count aloud the objects on the cards.(N1, 2, 3)
- Adapt counting songs and rhymes for Autumn (see activity opposite). (N1)
- Cut out 30 conkers from brown card. With a small group take it in turns to roll a dice and collect conkers. The 'squirrel' who collects the most conkers is the winner. (N6, 9)

Knowledge and Understanding of the World

- Go outside and collect safe signs that Autumn has arrived (eg acorns, conkers, twigs with no leaves).

Look under stones. Are there any minibeasts? Inside discuss what happens to some creatures which hibernate such as squirrels and frogs. (K1, 2)
- In preparation for Week 2 bake some harvest bread (see activity opposite). Encourage children to describe what they see, smell and, where appropriate, taste. (NB Children with coeliac disease may not eat bread which contains gluten.) (K2, 3)

Physical Development

- Encourage children to make shapes with their bodies like animals going into hibernation. Ask them to scamper like squirrels and as you count to 10 they should slowly curl into a tiny ball ready to sleep for the winter. (PD1)

Creative Development

- Use powder paints to make paintings of Autumn. Encourage children to mix Autumn colours. (C3)
- Start a collaborative display of a tree in Autumn. Leaves can be made by drawing around children's hands on Autumn coloured paper and cutting them out. (C2, 3)

Activity: An Autumn finger rhyme

Learning opportunity: Developing a familiarity with numbers one to five.

Early Learning Goal: Problem Solving, Reasoning and Numeracy Children should say and use number names in familiar contexts.

Resources: None.

Organisation: Whole group.

What to do: Use a 'carpet time' to learn and enjoy this rhyme. After each verse count the fingers which the children are holding up to reinforce number awareness.

- 5 red squirrels bushy and sweet, (hold up fingers of one hand)
- Are looking for some nuts to keep, (Hand in front of eyes - looking all around)
- One red squirrel climbs a tree (Mime climbing)
- Shuts his eyes and falls asleep,(Pretend to be asleep)
- So that leaves four red squirrels (clap, clap, clap, clap, then hold up 4 fingers ready for next verse)

Activity: Baking bread

Learning opportunity: Describing experiences using a variety of senses.

Early Learning Goal: Knowledge and Understanding of the World. Children should find out about... events they observe. They should look closely at similarities and differences... and change.

Resources: See recipe.

Organisation: Small group.

Key vocabulary: Bread, flour, water, yeast, sugar, salt, dough, knead, rise, bake.

What to do:
Recipe: For a dozen rolls:
3 teaspoons of dried yeast
600ml (1 pint) warm milk
900g (2lb) strong flour
2 teaspoons salt

Sprinkle the yeast on the milk and leave in a warm place for 15 minutes until frothy.

Put the flour and salt in a bowl. Make a well in the centre and pour in the yeast and milk mixture. Mix well to make a dough.

Turn onto a lightly floured surface and encourage the children to knead it well for several minutes. Put the dough in a clean bowl.

Cover with a clean tea towel and leave the dough in a warm place for about an hour until it has doubled in size.

Divide the dough into pieces for the children to use. They could make it into animal shapes, such as hedgehogs or crocodiles.

Leave the finished 'rolls' in a warm place for about half an hour before baking.

Bake at 230oC mark 8 for ten minutes, then 200oC, mark 6 for ten minutes. Cool on a rack.

As the children make the bread ask a variety of open-ended questions, encouraging children to use as many senses as possible. What does the flour feel like? Does the smell of yeast remind you of anything? What differences can you see after the dough has been left to rise? What can you smell as the bread bakes? What do you think of its taste?

Display

Cover a table with an Autumn coloured cloth. Display an Autumn picture in the centre. During the week add objects collected by the children which indicate the coming of Autumn. This display will be ongoing throughout the topic, gradually changing as themes progress. Display the collaborative 'Tree of Hands' in an area to which other trees can be added as seasons change.

Week 2
Harvest

Personal, Social and Emotional Development

- Talk about harvest as a time to say thank you for foods we eat. As a group make a list of foods for which to say thank you. (PS10)
- Look at pictures of foods eaten or grown in different countries. Discuss similarities and differences. Have children eaten the foods? What do they taste like? (PS6)
- When artefacts made by children are added to the ongoing Autumn display, encourage children to treat them carefully. Talk about the need to respect the property of others. (PS13)

Communication, Language and Literacy

- Read the Enormous Turnip (any version, eg Ladybird) As a group retell the story. (L4, 7, 16)
- Set up the role play area as a grocer's shop or market stall using pretend foods. Encourage children to make labels for the different foods using pictures or writing. Use the shop to take on the roles of customers and shop keepers. (L17)
- Encourage children to make their first name's initial letter from salt dough (see recipe opposite). (L10)

Problem Solving, Reasoning and Numeracy

- When using salt dough introduce and reinforce comparative vocabulary - shorter, shortest, longer, longest. (N9)
- Through buying and selling in the role play area encourage children to use numbers up to 10 and to solve simple problems showing awareness of addition. (N1, 2, 3, 4)
- Look at bread products of different shapes, for example, a baguette, a tin loaf, some pitta bread or a roll. Talk about the different shapes of the breads. Cut a slice of each. What shapes are the slices? (N11)
- Encourage children to make price tags for the foods in the role play shop, for example, apple - 4 pence. (N4)

Knowledge and Understanding of the World

- Closely observe a range of common vegetables and fruits. Sort according to shape and colour. (K1, 2, 3)
- Use salt dough to make models of common fruits and vegetables (see activity opposite). (K1, 3)

Physical Development

- Talk about harvesting and the types of machines farmers use to harvest. Ask children to mime being harvesting machines. Help them to discuss what they are harvesting and how the machine works. Encourage big movements at varying speeds and levels. (PD1)
- Play the shopping game (see activity opposite). (PD1, 4)

Creative Development

- Encourage children to make baskets from paper bun cases. Add a paper strip handle. Fill the baskets with harvest gifts made from scrap materials or dough or by cutting out pictures of foods from magazines. (C2, 3)
- Make up a dance showing the change from seed to harvest. (C5)

Activity: Salt dough models

Learning opportunity: Investigating the properties of dough and developing language to describe observations.

Early Learning Goal: Knowledge and Understanding of the World. Children should look for similarities (and) differences... They should investigate... materials by using all of their senses as appropriate.

Resources: Session 1: prepared dough, table covered with plastic cloth tall enough for children to stand to work. Session 2: paints in fruit colours.

Organisation: Up to 8 children.

Key vocabulary: Squash, stretch, squeeze, sticky, soft, hard.

What to do: Prepare some dough according to the following recipe:

2 cups plain flour
1 cup salt
1 tablespoon cooking oil
1/4 cup lukewarm water

Mix together the flour and salt. Add the oil and water and knead thoroughly.

NB Children with broken skin (such as open cuts or eczema) on their hands should not work with salt dough without protection from disposable surgical gloves.

Use a floor covering so that children may be involved in the preparation of the dough without worrying about too much mess. Talk about the textures of the flour and salt and the changes which happen as the liquid water and oil are added.

Provide each child with a ball of dough. Ask them to describe what it feels like. How can they change its shape? Can they roll the ball into a long sausage?

Show a range of common fruits. Discuss what they look like. Ask children to use their dough to make a model of one of the pieces of fruit.

After the models have been baked, talk about the changes which have happened. How has the dough changed?

Encourage children to paint their fruit being careful to match colours.

Activity: The shopping game

Learning opportunity: Working together collaboratively, listening to instructions.

Early Learning Goal: Physical Development. Children should move confidently and imaginatively with an awareness of space and others. They should show awareness of space, of themselves and of others.

Organisation: Whole group either outside or in a hall where the children can run. Children should sit in a large circle.

Key vocabulary: Apple, plum, pear, carrot, potato, bread, words to indicate ways to move.

What to do: Allocating the name of an item of food from the key vocabulary list to each child in the circle (up to 4 children could be each item).

Tell a story about Mrs Brown going shopping for food to fill a harvest basket. Include a mention of the different foods in a variety of ways, for example 'along the way Mrs Brown was tempted by the juicy red apples and she could not resist eating one of them; Just as she was about to go home she realised she had not got enough plums to make the jam...' As children hear their food word they stand up and move round the circle in a clockwise direction and sit down when they get back to their place. Additional instructions can be given in story form to indicate to the children how they should move, for example, the potatoes made Mrs Brown's bag so heavy that she was struggling to walk; the bread shop was about to close so she hurried along.

Display

Display the salt dough fruits in a large basket and add to the Autumn table.

Make a thank you display. Make a large 'Thank you' label to display on a table and invite children to think about the types of food for which they want to say thank you. Ask them to make models of this food with playdough, draw pictures or bring in food wrappers or labels to add to the display during the week.

Week 3
Autumn Leaves

Personal, Social and Emotional Development
- Provide opportunities for children to share and take turns when printing with leaves. (PS8)
- Use scissors with a zig-zag cutting edge to cut out a variety of shapes and colours of Autumn leaves. Cut each leaf into two. Give pairs of children a handful of leaf pieces. Encourage them to work together to match the pieces. (PS7)

Communication, Language and Literacy
- Look at a collection of Autumn leaves. Ask children to suggest words which describe their shape, colour, texture and sound. Write the words on a large leaf-shaped piece of paper. (L7, 8)
- Make a collection of things which begin with the sound 'l'. Provide each child with an 'l' shaped piece of paper. Ask them to fill the letter with drawings or pictures from mail order catalogues of objects which begin with that sound. (L10)
- Set up the role-play area as a tree house. Provide a range of glove puppets of animals which live in trees. (L1)

Problem Solving, Reasoning and Numeracy
- Sort Autumn leaves according to their shape, colour, size and edges. (N11)
- Make repeating leaf patterns. (N10)
- Repeat the conker game from Week 1 but with paper leaves. As a variation make a dice with any six numbers from 1 to 10. (N2, 3)

Knowledge and Understanding of the World
- Show children pictures of trees common to your local area. Discuss what the leaves on two of the trees look like. Go outside and try to find leaves for the two trees. Inside, use coloured chalks to make close observational drawings of the leaves. In a well ventilated area, away from children, spray the finished pictures with fixative or hair spray to prevent smudging. (K2, 3)
- Prepare a collection of 'half leaf' templates, and some folded pieces of A4 paper in a range of autumn colours. Show the children how to lay the template along the paper fold. Draw around it and cut along this line to make a complete leaf. Add them to the collaborative display (see below). (K2)

Physical Development
- Press leaves firmly into self-hardening clay which has been pre-cut into round or oval shapes. Allow to dry and display next to the original leaves. (PD8)
- Leaf printing (see activity opposite). (PD8)

Creative Development
- Use Autumn leaves to make pictures of animals seen in the Autumn. (C3)
- To the tune of London bridge is falling down sing 'Autumn leaves are falling down'. Further verses could include 'As we walk we rustle leaves', 'With a rake we gather them'. Encourage children to mime to the words or to provide percussion sound effects. (C5)
- Make a role-play tree house (see activity opposite). (C4)

Activity: A role-play tree house

Learning opportunity: Taking part in role play as groups and as individuals.

Early Learning Goal: Creative Development. Children should use their imagination in... role-play...

Resources: A corner of the room, two low tables or stage blocks, strong string or strong tape, a huge cardboard box (one from a fridge or cooker would be ideal) or a tall roll of corrugated card, green paper, brown and green paint, decorating paint brushes. Old shirts or coveralls for children. 'Home' play equipment such as rugs, tea sets.

Organisation: Involve as many children as possible, a few at a time.

Key vocabulary: Build, paint, tree trunk, leaves, branches, tree house.

What to do: This tree house uses low tables or stage blocks as a platform which allows children to pretend that they are high in a tree house.

Fix the two low tables very securely together using strong string or heavy duty tape such as duct or gaffer tape. Push the tables into a corner to make a raised square platform. Open out the cardboard box and use it to wrap around the tables forming a surround. Mark the places where the table legs are behind the card surround. Make small holes either side of the table legs and thread string through to tie the card in place. Repeat two or three times for each table leg to hold the card very securely. Cut a large entrance hole at table top height.

Now provide children with a large pot of brown paint, some decorators' brushes and some coveralls! Show them how to paint the outside of the card to look like a tree trunk. When the trunk is dry, encourage children to cut out lots of green paper leaf shapes and stick them around the top of the trunk.

Now invite the children to equip the inside of the tree house with home play equipment and to decorate the insides of the walls.

If necessary provide a safe step to help children to clamber in and out of their leafy house.

Activity: Leaf prints

Learning opportunity: Using materials with increasing confidence, control and dexterity.

Early Learning Goal: Physical Development. Children should handle tools (and) objects... with increasing control.

Resources: A selection of leaves, sponges, paint trays or paper plates, ready mix paint in autumn colours, newspaper, paper to print on.

Organisation: Small groups.

Key vocabulary: Sponge, paint, press, print.

What to do: Supply a paper plate or paint tray with a generous amount of paint and a sponge for each colour. Explain that using a separate sponge for each colour will prevent the colours from becoming mixed. Show how to dip the sponge in the paint and to wipe off the excess paint on the side of the plate or tray.

Show the children how to wipe the underside of a leaf with a painted sponge. The leaf is then placed onto the printing paper, painted side down.
Cover the leaf with a piece of newspaper and demonstrate how to gently press the leaf all over to ensure an even print.

Remove the newspaper and the leaf to see the results.

Display

Make a display of cut-out leaf prints mounted on coloured paper. Intersperse them with leaves of the types used for printing. Can children guess which type of leaf made each print?

Week 4
Autumn fruits

Personal, Social and Emotional Development

- Talk about fruits and berries and the danger of picking things we do not know are safe. (PS1, 2)
- Invite children to talk about their favourite fruits. Which fruit flavour drinks or ice creams do they prefer? Encourage children to listen carefully to the ideas of others, understanding that they may be different from their own. (PS2)
- Use snack time to share pieces of fruit, which have been prepared by an adult. NB Check for food allergies (PS8)

Communication, Language and Literacy

- Play an initial sound game in which children think about the initial sounds of the names of fruits. I went to the green grocer's and I bought a fruit beginning with ... (L9)
- Describe different fruits and ask children to identify them from a display. (L5)
- Place a fruit in a 'feely bag'. Encourage children to describe what they can feel and to identify the fruit. (L8)

Problem Solving, Reasoning and Numeracy

- Use conkers as non-standard units for measuring weight (see activity opposite). (N4, 9)
- Use this addition finger rhyme. (N2)

   Rustling through leaves on an Autumn day,
   (*Children mime walking through leaves*)
   I found a conker in my way.
   I picked it up and polished with delight
   (*Pretend to pick it up and polish*)
   My one brown conker(s) shined so bright.
   (*Hold up one finger*)
   Continue to two, three, four conkers and so on.

Knowledge and Understanding of the World

- Plant bulbs in preparation for Spring. (K1, 2)
- Use sunflower seeds, pips and so on to make pictures. Encourage children to look closely at the seeds and discuss what the seeds would grow into if they were planted. (K2, 3)
- Collect sycamore seeds. Encourage children to drop them and to observe and describe how they fall.

- Make paper gyros and observe how they spin like sycamore seeds (see activity opposite). (K4, 5, 6)
- Taste exotic fruits. (K1)

Physical Development

- Using balls and bean bags to represent Autumn fruits play games in which children are squirrels collecting nuts to store away. How many 'nuts' can children gather with one hand. Can they throw and catch the nuts? Can they throw the nuts into a bucket? (PD2, 7)
- Use climbing apparatus to be squirrels climbing trees. (PD1, 2, 7)

Creative Development

- Cut a selection of fruits in half and use them as printing blocks. Talk about the patterns which the fruit sections make. (C3, 5)
- Use tissue paper and textiles to make a collage of favourite fruits. Encourage children to talk about why they are their favourites and to match colours accurately. (C2, 3)

Activity: Sycamore seeds and paper gyros

Learning opportunity: Investigating the way sycamore seeds and paper gyros spin as they fall.

Early Learning Goal: Knowledge and Understanding of the World. Children should ask questions to gain information about why things happen.

Resources: Sycamore seeds, paper with gyros pre-drawn (see diagram).

Organisation: Groups of up to 4 children.

Key vocabulary: Sycamore seed, spinning, falling, wings.

What to do: Show children a sycamore seed. Discuss that it is a seed which comes from a sycamore tree. Drop the seed and ask children to describe the way it falls. Encourage them to notice the way it spins.
Show children how to cut out a paper gyro, bend the 'wings' and attach a paper clip to the end. Drop the gyro. Ask them what they notice.

Encourage children to investigate the paper gyros. What happens if they bend the wings the other way? What happens if they add more clips? Discuss how the gyros are similar to the sycamore seeds.

(NB Children should not stand on chairs to drop their gyros.)

Activity: Conkers as non-standard units

Learning opportunity: Using conkers as a means of measuring weight.

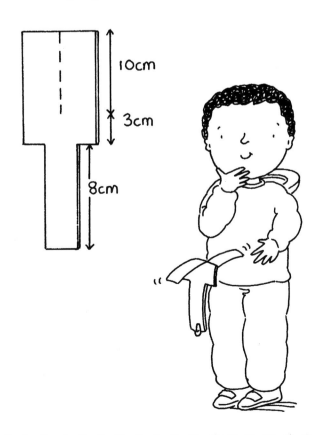

Early Learning Goal: Problem Solving, Reasoning and Numeracy Children should use their developing mathematical ideas to solve practical problems. They should use language such as... 'heavier' or 'lighter' to compare quantities

Resources: Collection of conkers, pan or bucket balances, soft toys.

Organisation: Children working in small groups.

Key vocabulary: Same as, more than, less than, balance, heavy, weight.

What to do: Invite children to handle a medium-sized soft toy. Talk about how they would describe the feel of the toy. Children will talk about its texture or the material it is made from. Encourage the conversation to a discussion of the weight of the toy. Would the children say it was heavy or light? How heavy? Explain that one way of describing how heavy something is, is to compare its weight to something else. The toy is as heavy as
....

Now introduce the conkers. Encourage the children to feel how heavy they are. Are they lighter or heavier than the toy? How many conkers do the children think would weigh the same as the toy?

Place the toy in one pan or bucket of a beam balance. Make sure the children understand the principal of how it works. How do we know when the objects in the two pans or buckets are the same weight? Relate the idea to children's experiences of playing on a see saw.

Invite children to balance the toy by placing conkers in the other pan or bucket. Encourage them to add conkers one or two at a time, watching for the buckets to balance. How will they know when they have added too many? How near were their guesses? What else could the children 'weigh' with conkers?

Display

Use the balancing with conkers activity to form the basis of an interactive display. Place the pan or bucket balances on a low table and provide conkers and a collection of objects to weigh.

Week 5
Windy week

Personal, Social and Emotional Development

● Tell the traditional story of the wind and sun arguing over who is strongest. Discuss the need to be sensitive to others feelings. Use the story as stimulus for role play (see activity opposite). (PS5, 6)

● Use jigsaws made from kite-shaped coloured card to encourage children to work together and to take turns. (PS8)

Communication, Language and Literacy

● Read The Wind Blew by Pat Hutchins (Picturemac). Collect words to describe the wind on a windy day. (L2, 4, 5)

● Read the poem 'Wind' from Out and About by Shirley Hughes (Walker Books). Encourage the children to talk about how it feels to be out for a walk in the wind. What sorts of things does the wind blow about? (L4, 12)

Problem Solving, Reasoning and Numeracy

● Make flags from straws and paper with numbers up to 10 on them. Encourage children to put them in number order. (N3)

● Provide a range of paper shapes from which children can make a triangular flag, a square flag and so on. (N11)

● Decorate kite-shaped pieces of paper. Encourage children to make tails for their kites in which the papers are arranged in a pattern eg red, yellow, red, yellow. (N10)

Knowledge and Understanding of the World

● Go outside on a breezy day with paper streamers. Encourage children to investigate how the wind blows the streamers. Hang up some of the streamers so they can be observed from inside. (K1, 2, 4)

● Attach sails made from straws, Blu-tack and paper to small plastic tubs. Float these in long seed trays or the water tray. Encourage children to investigate how the boats can be moved by blowing them. (K3, 4)

Physical Development

● Play a kite follow-my-leader game in which the children are a kite's tail. Use a large space in which the 'kite' can move in a variety of directions and at changing speeds. Explain that the tail is attached to the kite and that they must move exactly as the kite does. (PD1)

● Blow painting (see activity opposite). (PD8)

Creative Development

● Make shakers filled with a variety of seeds. Compare the different sounds they make. Investigate how one shaker can be played quietly and loudly. Use the shakers to simulate a soft breeze turning into a storm and then back to a breeze. Attach streamers to the shakers and use them for a wind dance. (C4, 5)

● Use finger painting to make swirling, windy patterns. (C3)

Activity: Wind and sun

Learning opportunity: Listening to a story and using it as focus for discussion and role play.

Early Learning Goal: Personal, Social and Emotional Development. Children should work as part of a group,... taking turns... They should be sensitive to the needs, views and feelings of others.

Resources: A cloak.

Organisation: Whole group sitting on the floor around the story teller.

Key vocabulary: Wind, blew, harder, sun, strongest, warm, hot, hotter.

What to do: Tell children the story of the sun discussing with the wind who is the strongest. They have a competition to see who can make a man take off the cloak he is wearing. First the wind blows harder and harder. The man just holds on tightly to his cloak. Then the sun shines down on the man. He becomes so hot that he takes off his cloak. The sun wins!

Talk about what the wind feels like when it blows. How can we tell how hard the wind is blowing? What do we feel like in the sun?

Who do children think won the competition? What does it feel like when we argue? What does it feel like to win or lose?

Ask three children to take on the roles of the sun, the wind and the man and enact the story. Encourage children to think about the feelings of the characters.

Activity: Blow painting

Learning opportunity: Using increasing control in using a 'blow' action to direct the flow of paint.

Early Learning Goal: Physical Development. Children should handle tools (and) objects... safely and with increasing control.

Resources: At least one drinking straw per child, runny paint (strong colours) in open tubs, a teaspoon for each colour of paint, paper.

Organisation: children working as individuals in a small group.

Key vocabulary: Blow, push, runny, liquid, blow hard, blow gently.

What to do: Show the children how to use a teaspoon to place a puddle of paint (about the size of a ten pence piece) in the middle of their sheet of paper. They are then going to make the paint spread over the paper by blowing it through the drinking straw.

To do this effectively they will need to blow 'along' the paint rather than down on to it, so the straw needs to be held at a low angle, almost parallel to the paper. Ensure

that the children understand the need to blow rather than suck!

As the children blow encourage them to talk about the patterns they are making. How can they make the paint travel more quickly or more slowly? How tiny can they make their 'branches' of paint?

Display

Make a display of the kites decorated by the children. Mount them against a blue background with white paper clouds and add, with children's help, some long tails with paper bows.

Week 6
Autumn Gallery

NB In some areas activities have been included which relate to Bonfire Night. Clearly these should only be used where children have had experience of fireworks.

Personal, Social and Emotional Development

- Talk about the Autumn Gallery and how visitors will need to be shown round. Share out jobs for preparing food, making labels, and so on. (PS7, 8)
- Several of the activities in this section refer to fireworks. At all times the dangers of playing with fireworks should be emphasised. Many children will, however, have experience of safe enjoyment of fireworks in family or organised events. (PS10)

Communication, Language and Literacy

- Retell a story about a firework celebration ('Paddington and the Bonfire' in More About Paddington by Michael Bond). (L13)
- Ask children to suggest words to describe the way fireworks look and sound. Write the words on a large piece of paper in the shape of a firework (see activity opposite). (L5)
- Talk about art galleries. In galleries there are guides who help visitors to find their way around and who answer questions. They wear name labels. Provide each child with a label to write their name on and decorate. (L15, 18)

Problem Solving, Reasoning and Numeracy

- Encourage children to help with the mounting and putting up of the Autumn displays. Discuss the shapes of pictures and the size of mounts needed for them. (N4, 11)
- Use the displays as a focus for the development of positional language: Next to, above, between, below etc. Ask questions such as 'Whose picture is next to Lloyd's?' (N12)

Knowledge and Understanding of the World

- Cover apples with melted chocolate and decorate with popcorn, vermicelli etc. Encourage children to observe how the chocolate melts and sets. Why does it melt? (K3, 4)
- Use a variety of 'found' natural materials, such as fir cones, acorns, hazelnut cases or twigs, to make models. Incorporate some commercial materials such as cleaned feathers, sequins or pipe cleaners to add extra features. As the children work talk about the materials they are using. Where did they come from? (K1, 2, 5, 6)
- Make traditional bonfire food - gingerbread (see activity opposite). (K1, 3)

Physical Development

- Use a tambourine to simulate the sound of a firework being lit, slowly burning until it is a mass of sizzling sparks ending with a loud bang. Encourage children to move in time to the tambourine. They could begin as a small curled up ball, then be lit fireworks in which arms and legs move in rhythmic circles. On the bang children should jump as high as they can, land gently and curl once more into a ball. (PD1)
- Talk about Catherine wheels. Encourage children to use hoops to be Catherine wheels. They could try spinning the hoop around their waists or arms or simply use it for bowling and catching. (PD2)

Creative Development

- Make rockets from cardboard tubes to hang from the ceiling. (C2, 3)
- On black paper make splatter pictures of exploding fireworks. (C3, 5)
- Talk about colours which show up well at night. Cover card stars on both sides with glitter, shiny paper, sequins, etc and hang them up. (C2, 3)

Activity: Firework words

Learning opportunity: Contributing words to describe the appearance and sounds of fireworks to add to a collaborative frieze.

Early Learning Goal: Communication Language and Literacy. Children should extend their vocabulary, exploring the meanings and sounds of new words.

Resources: Pictures of fireworks exploding in the sky, pieces of black paper, chalks, pastels or bright paints, shiny collage materials, glue.

Organisation: Whole group discussion followed by children working as individuals.

Key vocabulary: Firework, explode, bright, sparkle, shine, words to describe the sounds and appearance of fireworks.

What to do: Ask who has seen fireworks. What kinds of fireworks were they? Did they make sounds? What did they look like when they were lit? Which fireworks were children's favourites?

Look at the collected firework pictures. What fireworks can they see? Talk about the kinds of fireworks which children may have seen and heard such as sparklers, rockets, Catherine wheels and Roman candles. Ask them to suggest words to describe how the fireworks looked, behaved and sounded?

Talk about the ways in which some fireworks are named : Golden Rain, Silver Fountain, Volcano, Space Rocket. Why do the children think these names were chosen?

Explain that they are going to make a large firework picture for the Autumn Gallery. Encourage each child to make a firework collage on their piece of black paper, using a range of sparkly materials.

Display all the pictures together to make one large frieze. Write examples of the words which children suggested to describe the appearance, sounds and names of the fireworks on labels and incorporate them into the display. Read the words back to the children pointing to them as you do so. Ask whether the children can think of any other words to add.

Activity: Making gingerbread

Learning opportunity: Experiencing mixing and handling materials with opportunities to make and discuss observations.

Early Learning Goal: Knowledge and Understanding of the World. Children should look closely at... change. They should investigate... materials by using all of their senses as appropriate.

Resources: Ingredients for recipe below, rolling pins, cutters, dried fruit to decorate.

Organisation: Children in groups of up to four with adult support.

Key vocabulary: Mix, pour, stir, roll, words to describe the appearance, texture and smells of the dough, before, during and after baking.

What to do:

For approximately 30 children:
750g (24 oz) plain flour
10ml (2 teaspoons) bicarbonate of soda
20 ml (4 teaspoons) ground ginger
250g (8oz) chopped butter
375g (12 oz) soft light brown sugar
120ml (8 tablespoons) golden syrup
2 eggs, beaten dried fruit to decorate

1. Mix the sifted flour, bicarbonate of soda and ginger in a large bowl.

2. Rub in the butter until the mixture is like breadcrumbs.

3. In a separate bowl beat the syrup into the eggs.

4. Stir this into the flour mixture.

5. Mix to a firm dough.

Make sure that everyone has washed their hands.

If possible allow the children to help to make the dough, encouraging them to talk about the feel, appearance and smell of each ingredient as it is added. How does the mixture change after each addition?

This dough can be squashed, pummelled, pinched and kneaded almost indefinitely. It is extremely good tempered!

Show the children how to roll the dough and to use the cutters to make shapes. Allow them to use their own ideas in using the fried fruit to decorate.

Place each child's finished gingerbread on a separate, named piece of baking parchment on a baking tray.

Bake in a pre-heated oven, 180°C, Mark 4, for ten minutes.

Cool on a rack, then enjoy tasting!

Bringing It All Together

The Autumn Gallery Introducing the Idea

Explain to the children that in a few days time you are going to hold an Autumn Gallery. Talk to the children about galleries and exhibitions, explaining what the words mean. Have any of the children ever been to a museum, or seen a gallery of children's work on a television art programme? The children are going to make a gallery of their work for visitors to enjoy.

The gallery can be prepared as part of a morning or afternoon session, with guests joining the children later to admire the exhibits and share some refreshments.

You will need to plan the sessions to allow time for producing work for display and other preparations. Explain to children right at the beginning of the topic that they are working towards a gallery, so that some work will be put away to be kept safely. If your usual practice is that all work is taken home at the end of each session, you will need to ask children whether you may keep their work until after the exhibition. Make sure that the children understand that all their work will be taken home eventually. Continue to allow some work to go home, saving just one or two 'special' pieces of work for each child. If necessary arrange with parents/carers for individual pieces to be returned to you for display. It is important that children retain 'ownership' of their work.

Think about the work you have to show and how best to display it. It may fall into fairly clear categories or themes. If wall space is limited, flatwork can be displayed on garden trellis or large sheets of covered card. Models will need a table or large covered box. Think about combining 2-D and 3-D work, and use boxes of different shapes to make plinths, which children can help to cover and decorate. Keep a checklist of items on display, making sure that every child has at least one contribution in the gallery.

Making Preparations.

The introductory discussion will have helped children to understand that there are plenty of jobs to be done.

Food

Depending on the time of day at which the event is taking place, you may decide to provide simple refreshments. Encourage the children to think about what sorts of food and drink might be appropriate. Use the gingerbread recipe to make biscuits for guests. To make a change from the original activity encourage the children to make the biscuits in different shapes such as Autumn leaves or fruits. Ask the children how they think the biscuits should be stored and served. Decorate paper plates or paper tray covers in Autumn colours and patterns.

Invitations

Encourage the children to think about the sort of information which an invitation needs to give. Talk about the importance of visitors knowing when to come, and for how long the gallery will be open.

How could the invitations be designed to show the Autumn theme?

Encourage children to be adventurous in their ideas.

As children produce cards it is useful to have photocopied information (using children's suggestions) to paste inside them.

Accessories

Involve the children in making labels for their work, including headings for different sections of the displays. Ask the children to help you to word the labels which will give some information about their work. What were these pictures about? What sort of paint did you use?

Remind the children that this information could be important. As guides in the gallery they may need to answer questions. Some information signs may be needed in the gallery. Will visitors know where to collect refreshments or how to find the toilets?

Make a Gallery Open /Closed sign to go on the door.

Resources

Resources to collect
- A few magazines with recipes or pictures of fruits and vegetables, or gardening catalogues.
- Conkers, sycamore seeds, cones, acorns.
- Examples of fruits, vegetables and breads.
- Baking materials and ingredients (see recipes).
- Seasonal posters and pictures eg Practical Pre-School Seasons Posters.

Everyday resources
- Boxes, large and small for modelling.
- Papers and cards of different weights, colours and textures available eg sugar, corrugated card, silver and shiny papers.
- Dry powder paints for mixing and mixed paints for covering large areas such as card tree trunks.
- Different sized paint brushes from household brushes to thin brushes for delicate work and a variety of paint mixing containers.
- A variety of drawing and colouring pencils, crayons, pastels, charcoals.
- Additional decorative and finishing materials such as sequins, foils, glitter, tinsel, shiny wool and threads, beads, pieces of textiles, parcel ribbon.
- Table covers.

Stories
- *More About Paddington* by Michael Bond (Silverdale Books).
- *Titch* by Pat Hitchins (Red Fox).
- *Elmer and the Wind* by David McKee (Red Fox)
- *The Tale of Squirrel Nutkin* by Beatrix Potter (Penguin Books).
- *The Gingerbread Man* traditional story (Ladybird published a version).
- *The Prickly Hedgehog, The Sleepy Dormouse, The Hungry Otter, The Frightened Little Owl* by Mark Ezra and Gavin Rowe (Little Tiger Press): four countryside tales with evocative paintings, each set in a different season of the year.

Poems
- *This Little Puffin* by Elizabeth Matterson (Puffin).
- *Out and About* by Shirley Hughes (Walker Books).
- *Down the Lane: Sights and Sounds through the Seasons* by Valerie Greeley (Happy Cat Books).

Non-fiction
- *The Seasons* by Debbie MacKinnon (Frances Lincoln).

Information for Adults
- *The Early Years Foundation Stage: Setting the Standards for Learning, Development and Care for Children from Brith to Five* (Deparment for Children, Schools and Families).
- *Planning for Learning Through The Weather* Rachel Sparks Linfield and Penny Coltman (Practical Pre-School Books)

Home links

he theme of Autumn lends itself to useful links with children's families. Through working together children and adults gain respect for each other and build comfortable and confident relationships.

Establishing Partnerships

- Keep parents informed about the topic of Autumn, and the themes for each week. By understanding the work of the group, parents will enjoy the involvement of contributing ideas, time and resources.
- Request parental permission before taking children out of the group on an Autumn walk. Describe your route and the purposes of the activity. Additional parental help will be necessary for this activity to be carried out safely.
- Photocopy the Parent's page for each child to take home.
- Invite friends, childminders and families to share the 'Autumn Gallery'.

Visiting Enthusiasts

- Invite a parent, carer or friend who is a keen gardener to come into the group to talk about Autumn jobs in the garden. Perhaps they could bring examples of vegetables or fruits they have grown to show to the children.

- Invite adults from other cultures to show children how some of the less familiar fruits and vegetables are used in traditional recipes.

Resource Requests

- Encourage contributions of Autumn 'finds' from family walks.
- Ask to borrow Autumn coloured fabrics or seasonal pictures which could be used for displays.

Preparing the Autumn Gallery

- Invite enthusiastic cooks to help during the activities involving gingerbread or chocolate apple making.

Parent's Page

We have been using the theme of Autumn to introduce your child to different areas of learning. To follow up your child's work here are some fun play activities that you might like to try at home.

Talking
- Tell your child about the things you enjoyed as a child in Autumn. Perhaps you enjoyed watching bonfires, playing with conkers on strings or flying a kite.
- Talk about the importance of not picking any of the Autumn fruits which children see in hedgerows unless an adult said that it is safe to do so.

Making
- Make a bubble mix by mixing half a cup of baby bubble bath with two cups of water. 'Blowers' can be made from twisted plastic covered wire or old plastic bangles held at the edges. Alternatively dip the open end of a small plastic plant pot into a bowl of mix, and then blow through the hole in the bottom. Any household item with 'holes' can be waved about to make a shower of tiny bubbles. Sieves, slotted spoons or strainers all work well.
- Blow bubbles outside and observe their movement. Talk about the shapes of the bubbles and the way they wobble and move. What colours can the children see in them? How does the breeze blow them along? What makes them burst?
- Make a simple weather chart with a space for each day. Encourage children to record the weather by adding a suitable drawing in each space.

Story Telling
- Visit your local library with your child to look at books which feature Autumn.
- Make up a story about how one windy day you were flying a kite. Imagine that the kite string broke. What adventures did the kite have? How did you get it back?

In the Kitchen
- Allow your child to help in making a fruit pie. Encourage weighing, playing with pastry offcuts or making a pastry decoration for the middle of the pie.
- Draw attention to the changes which take place in the pastry and the fruit as the pie is baked.

Out and About
- As you walk or drive with children draw their attention to seasonal changes. Point out Autumn colours in the trees or the appearance of Winter stock in shops. Show children how leaf shapes can be used to identify trees. (See examples.)
- If you have a kite, enjoy flying it together! Talk about how the feel of wind tugging at the kite. Discuss which places are safe for flying kites.

What will children have the opportunity to learn
- to experience handling different materials;
- to make up stories and use their imagination;
- to recognise seasonal changes;
- to ask questions, investigate and explore.

Skills overview of six-week plan for Autumn

Week	Topic Focus	Personal, Social and Emotional Development	Communication, Language and Literacy	Problem Solving, Reasoning and Numeracy	Knowledge and Understanding of the World	Physical Development	Creative Development
1	Detecting Autumn	Caring for the environment	Making comparisons; Describing	Counting	Making observations	Changing body shapes	Painting; Cutting
2	Harvest	Appreciation; Sensitivity to others	Re-telling stories; Role-play; Initial sounds	Numbers to ten; Describing size and shape	Making observations; Sorting	Miming	Making a dance; Working in 3D
3	Autumn leaves	Sharing and taking turns	Role-play; Initial sounds	Describing shape and pattern; Counting	Recording observations; Looking at plants	Modelling; Controlling movement	Singing; Making rubbings
4	Autumn fruits	Talking about safety; Listening and sharing	Describing and identifying; Initial sounds	Using non-standard units; Addition	Growing plants	Throwing and catching; Climbing	Printing; Collage
5	Windy Week	Sensitivity to others; Working together	Describing	Ordering numbers 1-10; Shape and pattern	Describing and investigating the force of wind	Imitating movements; Blowing	Making sounds; Dancing; Painting
6	The Autumn Gallery	Sharing responsibility; Developing awareness of personal safety	Recognising names; Describing	Describing shape and position	Using materials	Moving imaginatively	Splatter painting; Using colour

WINTER

Topic Contents

Week 1
Detecting Winter

Personal, Social and Emotional Development

- Look at a large picture of a Winter scene (trees with no leaves, people dressed in warm clothes, people skiing and skating). Discuss what children like to do in Winter. Talk about how they feel in the Winter. What are their favourite activities? What do they do when it is dark in the evenings and they cannot play outside? (PS2, 3, 5)
- Discuss festivals which children in the group celebrate during Winter. Invite parents to come and talk to children about the celebrations. (PS6)

Communication, Language and Literacy

- Make a collaborative big book about Winter (see activity opposite). (L11, 19)

Problem Solving, Reasoning and Numeracy

- Choose a Winter theme for a display to reinforce awareness of a chosen number. For example if the number chosen is five, make a display showing the numeral 5, and a variety of collections of five objects: snowflakes, snowmen, winter hats, robins and so on. Involve different groups of children in creating each collection to contribute to the display. (N1, 2, 3)
- Use a collection of Winter objects or pictures to reinforce positional language (see activity opposite). (N12)

Knowledge and Understanding of the World

- On a walk look for signs that Winter is coming/has come. Show the children that some trees no longer have leaves. Look under stones for any remaining minibeasts. Look for birds and talk about ones which have flown away until the Spring. (K1, 2)
- In small groups go outside and ask children to pick out wintry scenes. Help the children to take photographs with a digital camera. (To maintain interest try to have them printed quickly!) (K1, 2, 9)

Physical Development

- Pretend to be very cold. What can we do to get warm? Play an action game based on a traditional favourite: 'Simon says keep warm by..... running on the spot, clapping, stamping, blowing on hands, rubbing hands, rubbing toes' and so on. Encourage children to listen carefully - remember that if the instruction does not begin with 'Simon says', it should be ignored! (PD 1, 2, 4)

Creative Development

- Use runny paint to 'blow' winter trees. Show the children how to use a brush to place a large blob of runny paint at the bottom of a piece of paper. Provide each child with a straw and show them how to hold the straw at a low level, almost horizontal and blow the paint along. Changing the direction of the blowing will produce forks in knobbly branches as the Winter tree grows. (C2)
- Prepare pictures for a group Winter book. (C5)
- Use blue, white and black paint to make as many shades and tones as possible. Ask children to cover a 30 x 30cm piece of paper. When completed mount the squares together to form a Winter patchwork. (C3)

Activity: The object line

Learning opportunity: Developing and reinforcing the use of positional language within the context of Winter.

Early Learning Goal: Problem Solving, Reasoning and Numeracy. Children should use everyday words to describe position.

Resources: A collection of objects associated with Winter, such as a paper snowflake, a sarf, a plastic robin, a mitten and a toy snowman. A selection of Winter pictures mounted onto A4 cards (if possible one per child).

Organisation: Whole or part group, carpet-time activity.

Key vocabulary: Positional language such as 'next to', 'between', 'behind', 'in front of'.

What to do: Show the collection of Winter objects to the children. Talk about each one and make sure that the children are familiar with them.

Place the objects in a row. Use positional language as you talk about the line. 'The snowman is next to the robin. The scarf is between the snowflake and the mitten.' Use questions to encourage children to use the same language. 'What is next to the scarf?', 'What is between the snowflake and the snowman?'

Give each child a prepared card to hold and ask the children to stand in a row. Ask them to describe their positions. 'Who is next to the Snowman picture?' 'Who is between the reindeer and the bird table?'

To extend the activity, see if children can move into the right places 'Can you make the snowman be between the cracker and the woolly hat?' Ask the children to stand in a line, one behind the other, so you can include the language of 'in front of' and 'behind'. This can become quite demanding: 'If the snowman and the scarf change places, who will be next to the reindeer?'

Activity: A Winter book

Learning opportunity: Drawing and writing about their own ideas as children work together to make a book.

Early Learning Goal: Communication, Language and Literacy. Children should use their phonic knowledge to write simple regular words and make phonetically plausible attempts at more complex words. They should use a pencil and hold it effectively to form recognisable letters, most of which are correctly formed.

Resources: A big book; blue sugar paper; chalks; hair-spray or commercial fixative spray; larger paper; card; staples or a needle and wool.

Organisation: Whole group introduction followed by small group work over the following days.

Key vocabulary: Book, cover, page, words, pictures, title, author.

What to do: Look at some big books. Show the children where the author's name is and talk about the cover. As you read the book draw attention to the illustrations. Explain to the children that they are going to work together to make a big book of their own. Each child is going to draw a Winter picture which will become part of this special book.

Working in small groups, provide each child with a piece of A4 blue sugar paper and chalks with which to draw. Encourage children to talk about their experiences of Winter and to develop their own ideas about what to draw. Scribe a sentence at the bottom of each picture to record the ideas expressed. To prevent the chalks from smudging, take the pictures to a separate, well ventilated area away from the children, and spray with hair-spray or fixative.

Mount the pictures onto larger pieces of paper and staple or sew them together to make a book. Encourage children to help in preparing a front cover with title and group authorship.

Display

Display the Winter book, inviting children and group visitors to enjoy reading it.

Use the collection of winter objects to form the basis of a wintry interactive display to which children can contribute. Use labels to reinforce the positional language developed in the activity.

Week 2
Winter Foods

Personal, Social and Emotional Development

- In Winter it can be difficult for birds to find enough food to eat. Discuss what birds eat and how children could help to feed the birds. (PS5)
- Set up a bird table with the children. Talk about the need to place it where cats cannot disturb the birds. Make a rota for children to take it in turns to change the water. Talk about the need to wash hands after touching the bird table. (PS8, 11)

Communication, Language and Literacy

- Encourage children to talk about Winter foods they enjoy, eating. Make favourite menus (see activity opposite). (L17, 19)
- Set up the role play area as a Winter cafe. Provide a couple of low tables with table cloths, chairs, a counter, till, plastic crockery and cutlery, paper napkins and trays. Provide note pads and pencils to allow for emergent writing as orders are taken. Invite children's suggestions for a name for the cafe to be displayed. Use a blackboard and chalks to write a menu of 'Today's Specials' and prices. (L7,17)
- Read or tell the story of 'The Enormous Turnip'. (L3)

Problem Solving, Reasoning and Numeracy

- Sort a selection of Winter vegetables according to size and shape. (M4, 12)
- Sing the song 'Five fat sausages cooking in a pan' (in *Okki-tokki-unga*). (M1, 2)

Knowledge and Understanding of the World

- Make and use bird feeders (see activity opposite). (K5)
- Use a selection of Winter vegetables and paint to make vegetable prints. Compare the prints. Later in the week see whether children can match the prints to the vegetables. (K3)
- Bake bird biscuits (see activity opposite). (K5)

Physical Development

- As you talk through the making of a Winter vegetable soup, encourage children to act out the processes. These might include growing and pulling the vegetables, peeling and chopping them, adding water and seasonings, stirring and pouring the soup, and enthusiastic tasting! (PD1)
- Make up a vegetable soup movement game. Designate areas of a large space using large pictures of vegetables. The centre of the space is the pot of soup. Call instructions for children to follow: 'Hop to the carrots', 'Creep to the cabbages' or 'Jump into the soup!'. (PD1, 2, 4)

Creative Development

- Make snowflake biscuits. Prepare an icing sugar mix which needs to be fairly wet but not too runny. Show children how to use a teaspoon to drop some of the mix onto a rich tea biscuit. Before the icing dries, show children how to use a dropper to allow just one or two drops of food colouring to fall onto the icing. Watch beautiful snow flake patterns appear as the colouring soaks into the icing. (C3)
- Talk about pasta as a warm winter food. Provide a variety of pasta shapes as a collage material. Talk about the shapes. Some are tubes, some look like wheels or shells, and so on. (Pasta can be coloured, by mixing with a little food colouring and drying in a gentle oven.) (C3)

Activity: Wintry menus

Learning opportunity: Making menus using simple words and pictures.

Early Learning Goal: Communication, Language and Literacy. Children should attempt writing for various purposes. They should use a pencil and hold it effectively to form recognisable letteres, most of which are correctly formed.

Resources: A3-sized stiff paper folded into two; magazines with food pictures; scissors; crayons; felt pens; glue; pencils; sticky labels on which to write food names; an example of a real menu and, if possible, a child's version.

Organisation: Small group around a table.

Key vocabulary: A variety of words relating to food.

What to do: Talk to children about the kinds of things they like to eat on a cold, wintry day. What would their favourite lunch be? Why?

Show children an example of a real menu. Look at the way it is organised. Explain that they are going to make a wintry lunch menu. Some children may like to use pictures from magazines, some may wish to draw and others might copy words or ask for an adult to scribe for them. If words are written on sticky labels children can choose where to place them. Once made, the menus can be used as a stimulus for role play in a cafe.

Activity: Bird food and feeders

Learning opportunity: Talking about birds in the local environment. Using materials to make bird feeders.

Early Learning Goal: Knowledge and Understanding of the World. Children should build and construct with a wide range of objects.

Resources: Foil trays; ingredients for pastry and bird cake (see below); plastic drinks bottles; milk cartons; strong string.

Organisation: Whole group discussion. For practical work, small groups. Over the week small groups will make a variety of feeders and bird food.

What to do: Show children pictures of birds which can be seen in the local environment. Talk about when and where children have seen the birds. Introduce the idea of regularly feeding birds. Show children a shop bought feeder. How does it work? Explain that during the week small groups will prepare different feeders and food for the birds.

Group 1: Bird cake:
Mix together sunflower seeds, millet, currants, oatmeal, kitchen scraps and stale cake. Cover with melted fat.

When slightly cooled press into round, foil dishes. Once cool the cake can be hung up as a 'feeding bell' or placed on a bird table. (NB Due to the severe nut allergies suffered by some children, the bird cake should not include peanuts.)

Group 2: Bird biscuits:
Wholemeal pastry is excellent food for birds. Encourage children to describe the texture of the pastry as they roll it out. Use cutters of a variety of shapes to make the biscuits. Place the biscuits on a bird table. See which shapes the birds prefer.

Group 3: Feeders:
Use milk cartons or plastic drinks bottles to make feeders. Although children will not be able to cut the holes for the feeders they should be encouraged to say where the hole should be made and to give reasons for their designs. Hang the feeders from a suitable nail or branch.

Display

On a table display a range of books and pictures of birds which children might see during the Winter. Each day put out a large piece of white paper on which children can draw/record birds they see on the bird table or feeders. Encourage children to notice what the birds are eating. At the end of two weeks make the sheets into a large book and share it with the group.

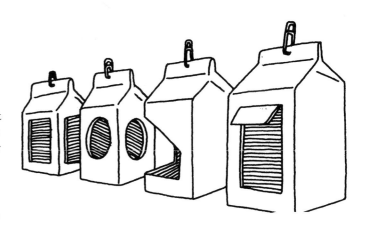

Week 3
Winter Weather-snow

Personal, Social and Emotional Development

- Talk about the need to handle other people's possessions with care. Talk about the snow storm display (see activity opposite) and using storms made by other children. (PS5)
- Read *Cuddly Dudley* by Jez Alborough (Walker) - a story about a penguin in the snow. Talk about brothers and sisters. How would the children feel if they were Dudley? (PS5, 10)
- Make a collection of picture books and pictures of animals which live in snowy areas. Talk to children about the animals. Make jigsaws from greetings cards picturing animals such as penguins and polar bears. Encourage children to work collaboratively to do the jigsaws. (PS8)

Communication, Language and Literacy

- Tell the children the story of *The Snowman* by Raymond Briggs using a version which does not have text (for example, Puffin). Point out that there is no text in this book; the pictures tell the story all by themselves. (L7, 8)
- Make name labels for the snow storm display (see activity opposite). (L18, 19)
- Make a collection of 'cold' words (freeze, snow, ice, cold, sparkle, white, shimmer). Cut six-pointed snowflakes from white or silver paper and display a word on each. (L5)

Problem Solving, Reasoning and Numeracy

- Provide each child with six snowmen holding hands cut from a piece of A4 folded white paper. Use the snowmen to develop: repeating pattern work - 'Colour alternate hats' (N10)
- number awareness - 'Give each snowman one nose, two eyes, and three buttons' (N1, 2)
- ideas of combination - 'Each snowman can have a red or blue hat, a green or yellow scarf, and an orange or carrot nose. Can you make each snowman different?' (N4)
- Make a dice-throwing 'beetle' game using snowmen. (N1, 2)

Knowledge and Understanding of the World

- Use a cornflour modelling dough - see activity opposite. (K1)

Physical Development

- Pretend to be a snowman melting on a hot day. (PD1)
- Use airflow balls or beanbags as imaginary snowballs. Practise catching and aiming. (PD7)
- Use white skittles or plastic bottles decorated as snowmen to practise aiming. (PD7)

Creative Development

- Make snowy 'spatter' pictures using white paint on black paper. For this you need brushes with short, firm bristles. (Old tooth brushes which have been sterilised are ideal.) Show the children how to dip the brush into the white paint and then to spatter paint onto the paper by either a sharp flicking action, or by running a finger towards themselves along the bristles. This takes practice and can be messy, but is highly enjoyable! Added interest can be achieved by laying templates onto the paper before splattering, and seeing the shape left as they are removed at the end of the activity. (C3)
- Make up a dance to the music from a video or audio tape of 'The Snowman'. (C5)
- Sing 'Jingle Bells'. (C5)
- Use desiccated coconut and/or glitter to make 'snowstorms' in see-through plastic bottles (see activity opposite). (C3)

Activity: Cornflower dough modelling

Learning opportunity: Exploring and manipulating a material as models are made.

Early Learning Goal: Knowledge and Understanding of the World. Children should investigate...materials by using all their senses as appropriate.

Resources: Recipe:
2 cups salt
1 cup cornflour

1 cup water (warm)
Colouring (optional)
Oil (optional)
Mix ingredients in a pan over a low heat, stirring well until texture becomes firm.

Organisation: Small group (Caution: children with eczema on their hands should avoid skin contact with any form of dough which contains salt. Surgical gloves should be provided for these children.)

Key vocabulary: Mix, dough, shape, mould, model, bake.

What to do: Cornflour dough is used in just the same way as a traditional salt dough. It can be used to make models which are then dried slowly in a gentle oven for several hours. The models will then keep more or less indefinitely. Cornflour dough has the advantage of being much softer than ordinary salt dough and so is easier for small children to use. It is also very white, which in this case enables it to be used to make mock 'snow' models, but which also makes it satisfying to paint. However, because it is not as stiff as salt dough, it is best to make shapes and models which lie flat.
The dough can be painted once it is dry. Alternatively several batches can be made and a different colour added to each during the cooking process.

Activity: Snow storms

Learning opportunity: Exploring texture and space.

Early Learning Goal: Creative Development. Children should explore texture...form and space...

Resources: Shop bought 'snow storm'; selection of safe snow-like materials such as desiccated coconut or glitter; old Christmas cards; clear plastic cups; sticky tape.

Organisation: Small group.

Key vocabulary: Shake, snowflake, fall, float, flutter, swirl.

What to do: Show children the shop bought 'snow storm'. Explain that they are going to make their own. Show them the snow materials. Do they remind the children of snow? How?

Half fill the cups with water. Put a spoonful of each snow material in each cup. Compare the way they float/fall. Gently swirl the cups. Talk about what happens.
Give each child a bottle. Ask them to cut a picture to be the scene for their snow storm. (The pictures can be stuck with tape around the bottle so that the picture can be seen through the bottle.)

Fill the bottles with water until they are three-quarters full. Invite each child to choose the material they want for their snow and put a dessertspoon in the bottle using a funnel. Screw the lid on tight - and shake!

Display
Cover a table with a white sheet. Place the snow storm bottles on the table. Add brief information labels which describe how the storms were made and invite friends and visitors to try them out.

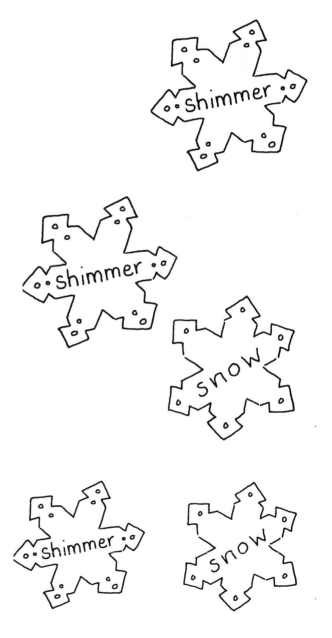

Week 4
Winter weather- ice

Personal, Social and Emotional Development
- Talk about the need to be careful when out and about in icy weather. Why can it be dangerous to play at sliding on icy paths, especially near a road? Why should children never try to walk over frozen ponds? (PS10)
- Tell the children about people who help us when the weather is icy, such as the men who drive gritting lorries through the night so that people can travel safely in the morning. (PS3)

Communication, Language and Literacy
- Discuss children's experiences of freezing and melting. What is an ice lolly like when it is frozen? What happens when it melts? What frozen foods do children like to eat? Talk about favourite varieties of ice lollies and ice cream. What is it that makes these special? Where should frozen foods be kept? Refer back to Raymond Briggs' story of 'The Snowman'. Why did the snowman like to sit in the freezer? Reinforce relevant language: freeze, frozen, melt, melting, thaw, ice, water, solid and liquid. Encourage children to use descriptive language as they describe their own experiences and preferences. (L7, 8)
- Pass around an imaginary ice lolly. What does each child taste as they sample it? When does it begin to melt? (L1)

Problem Solving, Reasoning and Numeracy
- Use the ice cube counting rhyme (see activity opposite). (N1)
- Use lolly sticks to make patterns and shapes. Talk about the names of 2-D shapes as they are made, introducing the words triangle, square and oblong. Can children use lolly sticks to make a house shape? How many sticks do they need? (N11)

Knowledge and Understanding of the World
- Talk about the need to wear shoes which grip well when it is icy. Make wax crayon rubbings of shoe soles. Compare the patterns. Which do children think have the best grip? (K1, 3)
- Make and melt coloured icebergs (see activity opposite). (K3)

Physical Development
- Play a variation on the game of musical statues. Before playing music, each time give a different instruction about the shape into which the children are to 'freeze': a spiky shape, a round shape, a wide shape and so on. (PD1, 2)
- Use sliding apparatus, reinforcing language of slipping and sliding. Older or more able children will be able to slide in different ways, sitting, lying and so on. (PD7)

Creative Development
- Encourage children to think about words they could use to describe the appearance of trees on an icy or very frosty day. Provide children with large twig shapes pre-cut from dark paper and a selection of scraps of white, sparkly and shiny materials. Examples might include small strips of polythene, silver and white glitter, tinsel, foil, silver buttons or sequins. (C3)
- Use simple percussion instruments to talk about sounds which remind children of cold, icy weather. Use metallic instruments such as triangles, Indian bells and glockenspiels to compose a collaborative 'icy symphony'. (C4)

Activity: Ice cube rhyme

Learning opportunity: Using a counting rhyme for numbers five to one.

Early Learning Goal: Probem Solving, Reasoning and Numeracy. Children should say and use number names in order in familiar contexts.

Resources: None.

Organisation: Whole group sitting comfortably on the floor in a circle.

Key vocabulary: Freeze, frozen, melt, thaw, solid, liquid.

What to do: Talk about ice. What happens to it when it is left in a warm room? Check children understand the word 'melt'. Teach the group the rhyme with the actions:
Five cubes of freezing ice, (*Hold up five fingers*)

To make my drink cold and nice.

Now I drop one in my squash, (*Mime dropping one into a drink*)

Splash it goes, splish, splosh! (*Clap on 'splash', slide hands together for 'splish, splosh'*)

Slowly my cube melts away,

I've got four for another day. (*Hold up four fingers*)

Four cubes........

As children become more confident with the rhyme it can be changed to start with different numbers of cubes and by using two cubes in some of the drinks. This will encourage children to listen to the rhyme and to be observant as varying numbers of fingers are put down

Activity: Make a giant iceberg

Learning opportunity: Observing, describing and recording changes as ice melts.

Early Learning Goal: Knowledge and Understanding of the World. Children will be able to look closely at similarities, differences, patterns and change.

Resources: Coloured water; large container; water tray.

Organisation: Small group.

Key vocabulary: Float, sink, smaller, bigger.

What to do: Colour some water using food colouring and freeze it in a large container. A plastic bucket or ice cream box is ideal for this purpose, large jelly moulds are even better.

Remove all the toys from the water tray and fill it with warm water. Explain to the children that you are going to put the frozen coloured 'iceberg' into the water. What do they think will happen? Will it float or sink?
Once the iceberg is in the water, encourage the children to watch carefully. What happens to the rest of the water in the tray? Where has this colour come from? How does the iceberg change?

Some children may enjoy recording their observations in the form of drawings or paintings. Photographs are also a useful way of recording this experience for children to share later with friends and family members.

Display
Display the decorated frosty branches with a variety of the words which children used to describe their ideas and experiences of icy weather.

Week 5
Winter Clothes

Personal, Social and Emotional Development

- Talk about the importance of looking after clothes properly, hanging coats on pegs, keeping shoes and socks in pairs and so on. Begin an 'I can.....' chart with each child. Challenges could include fastening shoes, putting on gloves, folding clothes and so on. Ensure all children are able to record some 'I cans'. (PS11)

  Have a winter dressing-up area. Provide small groups of children with a selection of Winter dressing-up clothes. Include mittens, scarves and hats. Who can dress themselves for an imaginary winter walk? (PS11)

Communication, Language and Literacy

- Talk about getting dressed for a Winter walk (see activity opposite). (L8)
- Encourage recognition of letter sounds by playing a game. 'I'm thinking of something to wear, and it begins with the sound....'. (L9)

Problem Solving, Reasoning and Numeracy

- Prepare a selection of pairs of gloves, mittens, boots, hats and scarves from coloured paper or card. Encourage children to sort them into pairs and to place them in groups according to colour and to shape. (N11)
- Use the gloves, mittens, boots, hats and scarves to make repeating patterns for the children to continue (for example, red glove, blue hat, green scarf, red glove.....). (N10)
- Provide each child with a photocopy of a scarf divided into about 12 sections. Encourage them to colour the scarves in repeating patterns. (N10)

Knowledge and Understanding of the World

- Winter evenings are dark. Discuss what sorts of clothes are easy to see in the dark. Show children a range of reflective items which cyclists might wear to be easily visible. Provide each child with a paper armband to cover with reflective sequins or shiny scraps that would be easy to see at night. (K1, 4)
- Make a winter washing line (see activity below). (K1)

Physical Development

- Hold a winter dressing-up race. (PD2, 7)

Creative Development

- Use mail order catalogues for children to cut up and select their favourite Winter outfit. Later, encourage children to paint self-portraits, modelling their choices. (C3)

Activity: Winter washing line

Learning opportunity: Describing and selecting materials.

Early Learning Goal: Knowledge and Understanding of the World. Children should investigate... materials by using all of their senses as appropriate.

Resources: A variety of collage materials, wool scraps and textiles. Pre-cut shapes of Winter garments on thin card, about A4 in size.

Organisation: Small group.

Key vocabulary: Warm, thick, soft, fluffy, smooth, shiny.

What to do: Talk to the children about how they would describe their Winter clothes. What sorts of clothes are fluffy, soft, smooth, waterproof, shiny or warm? Provide each child with a pre-cut shape and encourage them to decide what word would best describe that garment. A jumper might be 'fluffy' and a mackintosh 'smooth'. This word is going to be the theme of their individual collage.

Younger or less able children will need support and guidance as they select materials with which to cover their shape. Constantly reinforce the chosen adjective. Which of the materials on the table could be described in this way? Allow more able children to discriminate between materials, discussing their ideas as they make selections.

Display each completed collage garment, together with its relevant describing word, on a washing line display.

Activity: Getting dressed

Learning opportunity: Developing sequencing skills as an everyday experience is described.

Early Learning Goal: Communication, Language and Literacy. Children should use talk to... sequence...events.

Resources: Selection of outdoor Winter clothes.

Organisation: Whole group.

Key vocabulary: First, next, last, pull, push.

What to do: Use the process of getting ready for a Winter walk to develop sequencing skills. In what order are outdoor clothes put on? What would happen if we put clothes on in the wrong order?

Talk about how we pull a jumper over our heads, but push our arms into the sleeves. We pull up socks, but push our feet into boots. What other clothes do we push or pull? Encourage children to mime the actions as they think about putting on a variety of warm clothes.

Display
Make a display of Winter clothes labelled with names and describing words.

Planning for Learning through The Seasons

Week 6
Winter fair

Personal, Social and Emotional Development
● Talk about handling food. Why is it important to have very clean hands and equipment? (PS10, 11)
● Discuss how visitors to the group will be welcomed and cared for. (PS5, 8, 13)
● The fair may become a crowded event. Talk about safe behaviour. (PS10)

Communication, Language and Literacy
● Talk to the children about making posters to advertise the Winter fair. What information will people need? Scribe children's ideas onto large pieces of paper and then invite them to add decorations to make the posters attractive. (L17)

Problem Solving, Reasoning and Numeracy
● Use food preparation as an opportunity to develop understandings of shape and number. What shapes are the biscuits? How could we cut sandwiches into triangles, squares or oblongs? How many slices should each cake be cut into? (N4, 11)
● If you are going to charge for games or activities children will need individual adult support in handling money. However, it is helpful to talk to children about different coins, naming each one and describing its shape, colour and size. Do not expect young children to be ready to be able to count money or to understand about giving change. (N3, 11)
● Children can help you to prepare a 'Guess the number' game. This is a useful opportunity for children to encounter large numbers, as they help you, for example, to count sweets into a jar. (N4)

Knowledge and Understanding of the World
● Make Winter vegetable soup (see activity below). (K3)
● Talk about the need to decorate the room, stalls and games for the Winter fair. Encourage children to contribute by making paper chains, crepe paper fringing, paper doilies or cut-out shapes to enhance the produce/game. Encourage children to ask questions about methods and materials they might use. (K6)

Physical Development
● Practise games which will be played at the fair. (PD1, 2)
● Enjoy role-play when out on a wintry day (see the activity opposite). (PD1)

Creative Development
● Make a find-the-treasure game based on a snow scene. (C3, 5)
● Make a Winter wishing well from a large box and a bucket for people to donate loose change in at the fair. Decorate it with paper icicles and glitter. On the well write:
'As you wish, shut your eyes,
Hoping for a nice surprise.
It might come true or it might not
But it will help *................... such a lot!'
* *insert name of group or charity*
(written by Jessica Ray aged 9) (C3)

Activity: Winter soup
Learning opportunity: Observing cooked and uncooked vegetables, cutting vegetables.

Early Learning Goal: Knowledge and Understanding of the World. Children should look closely at differences, similarities...and change.

Resources: Large saucepan; range of vegetables; two chopping boards; knives which are sharp enough to cut raw vegetables but safe for children to use; two vegetable stock cubes per pan of soup.

Organisation: Pairs of children.

Key vocabulary: Slice, chop, cook, simmer, boil, raw, cooked.

What to do: Talk to children about soup. What does it taste like? Which flavours are children's favourites? Many people like to eat soup in Winter because it warms them up on a cold day.

Explain that the group is going to make soup for the Winter fair. Show children the vegetables they are going to use. Can they name them? What do they look like? Help pairs of children under close supervision to chop a range of vegetables. Place the vegetable pieces in a large pan, cover with water and add two vegetable stock cubes. Save one piece of each vegetable for comparing with the cooked versions. Allow the soup to simmer for about half an hour. Cool to body temperature before serving to children. When cooked encourage children to compare the cooked vegetables with the raw pieces.

Activity: The wintry day

Learning opportunity: Listening and responding as a group in a role play context.

Early Learning Goal: Physical Development. Children should move with confidence, imagination and in safety.

Resources: None.

Organisation: Whole group in a large space.

Key vocabulary: Stamp, rub, slip, slide, stride.

What to do: Start with the children sitting comfortably on the floor. Talk about a wintry day. It is cold but the sun is shining. Ask them to imagine they are going to go to play outside. First they must get ready. Talk through the process of putting on outdoor clothes (linking back to 'Winter clothes' week), with children acting out the movements.

Describe going through the door and into the cold air. Now it is time to warm up! Use actions such as stamping, rubbing hands, swinging arms, clapping or jumping on the spot.

Ask the children to test carefully to see if the ground is slippery. Start in thin snow which gradually gets deeper and deeper, with walking becoming very slow with high steps. Children step over cracks in the snow with long, definite strides.

Suddenly it starts to snow. The children skip about catching the snowflakes. They play in the snow, making snowballs and building snowmen. Now the snow begins to fall very heavily. Walking is a great effort, pushing against the wind and wiping snow from eyes. Fortunately the storm does not last long and the children are soon able to skip back to their door.
Feet are stamped to remove snow and boots are pulled off. Outdoor clothes are removed (and put away!) and the children settle down to enjoy a warm drink.

Display

From the ceiling hang long, dangling streamers of white, grey and pale blue crepe paper interspersed with silver tinsel. Cover windows with pieces of pale blue and grey tissue paper. The overall effect should be to turn the group's room into a dreamy, Winterland ready for the Winter fair.

On a table put out a collection of shiny materials, metal spoons and plastic mirrors for children to explore reflections. Arrange cushions on the floor with a box of Winter picture books.

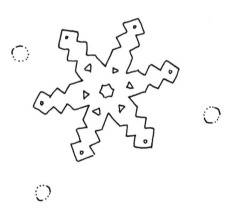

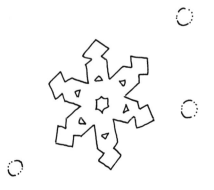

Bringing It All Together - Introducing the winter fair

Talk to the children about the Winter fair and its purposes. You may decide to use this as a fund-raising opportunity for the group or a charity, or you may prefer simply to prepare and enjoy the fun.

Brainstorm together ideas for things to make and games to play. Talk about the jobs you'll need to do to prepare for the fair and also the things which will need to be done on the day. Explain that this is something which you are going to prepare together. Everyone will have something to do.

Involving the children in preparations

The introductory discussion will have helped children to understand that there are plenty of jobs to be done.

Games to make:

- Pin (use Blu-tack rather than pins) the nose on the snowman.
- Guess the number of white bonbon sweets (snowballs) in a jar, or the number of sunflower seeds glued to a bird table picture.
- Throwing table tennis balls (snowballs) into a bucket.
- Guess the birthday of .... (a knitted snowman or toy penguin).
- Find-the-treasure game (Stick a flag on a snowy scene).

Items which could be sold

- Mugs of winter soup (not too hot!) made by the children will be welcome on a cold day.
- Salt dough fridge magnets are easy for children to make. Show them how to roll out the salt dough and to cut shapes using small biscuit cutters.

Once the models are dry they can be painted by the children and varnished by adults. Small button magnets, to glue to the back of each shape, are inexpensive and can be purchased from most craft shops.

If a group helper grows herbs in pots or a garden, dry a few sprigs to make wintry 'herb bags' to flavour winter soups and stews. You'll need some pre-cut circles of cheap muslin or cotton, about ten centimetres across. Show children how to lay a selection of dried herb sprigs in the centre and then gather up the fabric to make a little bag. The neck can be tied with string.

Accessories

Encourage children to help you choose names for the stalls and games, and to decorate banners and notices. If the fair is for fun only, you could make winners' certificates for the games.

Resources

Resources to collect :
- Clear containers for making 'snow storms'.
- A commercially produced 'snow storm'.
- A cloth in blue or other wintry colours to use as a display background.
- A large plastic tub or jelly mould for making an 'iceberg'.
- Bird table (optional).
- Clean milk cartons to make bird feeders.
- Marbling inks and trays.
- Drinking straws.

Everyday resources:
- Boxes, large and small for modelling.
- Papers and cards of different weights, colours and textures for example, sugar, corrugated card, silver and shiny papers and so on.
- Dry powder paints for mixing and mixed paints for covering large areas.
- Different sized paint brushes from household brushes to thin brushes for delicate work and a variety of paint mixing containers.
- A variety of drawing and colouring pencils, crayons, pastels, charcoals and so on.
- Additional decorative and finishing materials such as sequins, foils, glitter, tinsel, shiny wool and threads, beads, pieces of textiles, parcel ribbon.
- Table covers.
- Clear plastic cups and bottles.

Stories
- *Funnybones: The Black Cat* by Allan Ahlberg and Andre Amstutz (Puffin Books).
- *Cuddly Dudley* by Jez Alborough (Walker).
- *Little Polar Bear* by Hans de Beer (North-South Books).
- *The Snow* by John Burningham (Red Fox).
- The Cross Rabbit by Nick Butterworth (Picture Lions).
- *The Winter Hedgehog* by Ann and Reg Cartwright (Red Fox).
- *Jolly Snow* by Jane Hissey (Red Fox).
- *Penguin Pete* by Marcus Pfister (North-South books).
- *The Cat in the Hat Comes Back* by Dr Seuss (Collins).
- Little Penguin by Patrick Benson (Walker Books).
- *The Big Dark* by JOhn Procter (Red Fox).
- *Winnie in Winter* by Korky Paul and Valerie Thomas (Oxford University Press).

Poetry books
- *This Little Puffin: Finger Plays and Nursery Rhymes* by Elizabeth Matterson (Puffin).

Songs
- *Harlequin 44 Songs Round the Year* chosen by David Gadsby and Beatrice Harrop (A & C Black).
- *Okki-tokki-unga Action Songs for Children* chosen by Beatrice Harrop, Linda Friend and David Gadsby (A & C Black).

Resources for planning
- *Planning for Learning through the Weather* by Rachel Sparks Linfield (Practical Pre-School Books)
- *Planning for Learning through the 12 Days of Christmas* by Rachel Sparks Linfield (Practical Pre-School Books)
- *The Early Years Foundation Stage: Setting the Standards for Learning, Development and Care for Children from Birth to Five* (Department for Schools, Children and Families)

Home links

The theme of Winter lends itself to useful links with children's homes and families. Through working together children and adults gain respect for each other and build comfortable and confident relationships.

Establishing Partnerships

- Keep parents informed about the topic of Winter, and the themes for each week. By understanding the work of the group, parents will enjoy the involvement of contributing ideas, time and resources.
- Photocopy the Parent's page for each child to take home. This will give parents additional information which will enable them to support the topic through shared activities, encouraging children to be aware of seasonal changes in their environment.
- Invite friends, carers and families to attend the Winter fair.

Group Visitors

- Invite adults known to the children to come and talk to the children about childhood memories of Winter.
- Invite parents and friends to tell the children about their knowledge or experience of a variety of Winter traditions and celebrations.

Resource Requests

- Shiny scraps and old greetings cards will be useful materials to collect.

The winter fair

- Help will be needed in supporting children as they make their games. At the event it will be helpful to have additional adult helpers to assist children as they take charge of their games and stalls.

Parent's Page

We have been using the theme of Winter to introduce your child to different areas of learning. If you would like to follow this up at home, here are a few activities you might like to try. Play activities should be fun. Do not force your child to learn.

Talking
- Tell your child about the things you enjoyed doing in Winter as a child.
- Encourage them to see differences and similarities between the present and past.

Making
- Show your child how to make paper snowflakes. Although children may find the cutting out very difficult, they will enjoy colouring the flakes using felt pens, or adding sequins, shiny scraps or glitter to make decorations.
- Explain that although all snowflakes have six 'arms' there are no two snowflakes exactly the same, even in the thickest snow storm! If you have the opportunity, take a magnifier outside when snow is falling to investigate this.

Story Telling
- Visit your local library with your child to look for books which feature Winter.

- All children love listening to stories. Make up a story about your child enjoying a Winter adventure. These are especially effective if continued from day to day. Encourage your child to join in, helping you to decide on the events for each exciting installment.

In the Kitchen
- Talk about the different types of seasonal foods which we enjoy in Winter, as you prepare hot drinks or meals on a cold Winter's day. Draw attention to the smells of hot food. Why do we enjoy hot food in the winter?
- Emphasise the need to be careful when preparing or tasting hot foods.
- Make cakes, biscuits or sweets for the Winter fair.

Out and about
- We have been preparing bird food. Encourage your child to help the birds to survive through Winter by putting out fresh water and scraps, perhaps on a window ledge.
- Use opportunities to draw children's attention to signs of Winter: Winter clothes, bare trees, frosty mornings, icy puddles or the shorter days.

What will children have the opportunity to learn?
- to experience handling different materials;
- to make up stories and use their imagination;
- to recognise seasonal changes;
- to ask questions, investigate and explore.

Skills overview of six-week plan for Winter

Week	Topic Focus	Personal, Social and Emotional Development	Communication, Language and Literacy	Problem Solving, Reasoning and Numeracy	Knowledge and Understanding of the World	Physical Development	Creative Development
1	Detecting Winter	Appreciating the environment; Being sensitive to other	Collaborative early writing; Appreciating books	Counting; Developing positional language	Observing; Recording	Moving imaginatively; Increasing control	Handling materials; Painting
2	Winter foods	Treating living things with care and concern	Listening; Role Play; Talking; Early writing	Sorting; Number awareness	Comparing; Observing; Making	Moving imaginatively	Using a variety of materials; Glueing
3	Winter weather - snow	Being sensitive to others; Working collaboratively	Discussing; Writing; Enjoying stories and poems	Counting; Making patterns	Comparing; Observing	Imaginative movement; Aiming	Handling materials; Singing; Dancing
4	Winter weather - ice	Safety awareness	Language development	Counting; Shape and pattern	Observing; Comparing	Moving with imagination and control	Working with a variety of materials; Using instruments
5	Winter clothes	Looking after ourselves	Discussing; Recognising sounds	Sorting; Making patterns	Observing; Comparing	Fine motor skill development	Cutting and painting
6	Winter fair	Caring for others; Safety and hygiene awareness	Knowing that words and pictures carry meaning; Early writing	Recognising shapes; Number	Comparing; Observing; Questioning	Moving with control	Making for a purpose

Planning for Learning through The Seasons

Practical Pre-School Books   PHOTOCOPIABLE SHEET

Collecting Evidence of Children's Learning

Monitoring children's development is an important task. Keeping a record of children's achievements, interests and learning styles will help you to see progress and will draw attention to those who are having difficulties for some reason. If a child needs additional professional help, such as speech therapy, your records will provide valuable evidence.

Records should be the result of collaboration between group leaders, parents and carers. Parents should be made aware of your record keeping policies when their child joins your group. Show them the type of records you are keeping and make sure they understand that they have an opportunity to contribute. As a general rule, your records should form an open document. Any parent should have access to records relating to his or her child. Take regular opportunities to talk to parents about children's progress. If you have formal discussions regarding children about whom you have particular concerns, a dated record of the main points should be kept.

Keeping it manageable

Records should be helpful in informing group leaders, adult helpers and parents and always be for the benefit of the child. The golden rule is to keep them simple, manageable and useful.

Observations will basically fall into three categories:

- Spontaneous records: Sometimes you will want to make a note of observations as they happen e.g. a child is heard counting cars accurately during a play activity, or is seen to play collaboratively for the first time.
- Planned observations: Sometimes you will plan to make observations of children's developing skills in their everyday activities. Using the learning opportunity identified for an activity will help you to make appropriate judgments about children's capabilities and to record them systematically.

To collect information:

- talk to children about their activities and listen to their responses;
- listen to children talking to each other;
- observe children's work such as early writing, drawings, paintings and 3D models. (Keeping photocopies or photographs is sometimes useful.)

Sometimes you may wish to set up 'one off' activities for the purposes of monitoring development. Some groups at the beginning of each term, for example, ask children to write their name and to make a drawing of themselves to record their progressing skills in both co-ordination and observation. Do not attempt to make records following every activity!

Reflective observations:

It is useful to spend regular time reflecting on the children's progress. Aim to make some comments about each child each week.

Informing your planning

Collecting evidence about children's progress is time consuming and it is important that it is useful. When you are planning, use the information you have collected to help you to decide what learning opportunities you need to provide next for children. For example, a child who has poor pencil or brush control will benefit from more play with dough or construction toys to build the strength of hand muscles.

For examples of how to record developing skills across all four topics covered in this book please refer to the recording chart on the next page.

Example of recording chart

Name: Alice Field	D.O.B. 1.04.04			Date of entry: 22.4.08	
Term	**Personal, Social and Emotional Development**	**Communication, Language and Literacy**	**Problem Solving, Reasoning and Numeracy**	**Knowledge and Understanding of the World**	**Physical Development**	**Creative Development**
ONE - Spring Topic	Keen to see frog spawn change. Anxious to return to tadpoles to pond. 20.4.08 EHL	Enjoying listening to poems. Those by Shirley Hughes are particular favourites. 20.3.08 LSS	Was able to carry out addition by counting objects. 26.2.08 LSS	Interested in story of wool. Brought in knitted doll. 16.3.08 AC	Showed good control with blow painting. Finding balancing difficult. 16.2.08 AC	Enjoyed the challenge of weaving - showed great perservance. 2.3.08 LSS
TWO - Summer Topic	Starting to collaborate with peers. Prefers adult company. 1.11.08 EMH	Enjoys listening to stories. *Titch* a particular favourite. 19.10.08 EMH	Is able to say numbers to ten and count accurately five objects. Recognises halves and quarters. 03.12.08 SJS	Very keen on flowers. Brought in examples of pressed flowers from home, 19.10.08 EC	Can hop. Finds using ball difficult. 29.9.08 AC	Enjoys gluing and cutting. Made a wonderful model caravan. 7.12.08 LSS
THREE - Autumn Topic	Reluctant to say goodbye to mother. Prefers adult company. 20.9.08 EMH	Enjoying listening to stories. Hungry caterpillar a particular favourite. 20.11.08 EMH	Is able to say numbers to ten and count accurately five objects. Recognises and names squares and circles. 5.11.08 BM	Very keen on minibeasts. Brought in pictures from home. 16.10.08 AC	Can balance on one leg. Finds threading beads difficult 16.10.08 AC	Enjoys gluing and cutting. Made a wonderful Duplo castle. 20.10.08 LSS
FOUR- Winter topic	Quickly and independently dresses for outdoor play. Eager to help peers with shoes etc. Can tie loose bow. 20.1.08 EMH	Enjoying listening to stories. independently wrote 'Jon' for the group 'big book' 20.1.08 EHL	Is able to say numbers to ten and to count accurately five objects. Can recognise and complete simple repeating patterns. 5.3.08 SJS	Very keen to observe melting ice. Good use of vocabulary for describing observations. 16.2.08 LSS	Finds it hard to balance on one leg. Enjoys aiming at skittles. Starting to control speed and direction of ball. 16.2.08AC	Enjoys gluing and cutting. Made a wonderful winter colage. 20.3.08 LSS